GINGER

GINGER

The Ultimate Home Remedy

Dr Stephen Fulder

SOUVENIR PRESS

First published 1993 by Souvenir Press Ltd,
43 Great Russell Street, London WC1B 3PA
and simultaneously in Canada

Reprinted 1993

ISBN 0 285 63127 6

Cover drawing and diagram of chemical compounds
by Duncan Lowe

Photoset by Rowland Phototypesetting Ltd
Bury St Edmunds, Suffolk
Printed in Great Britain by
The Guernsey Press Co. Ltd., Guernsey, Channel Islands.

As they fell from heaven, the plants said,
'Whichever living soul we pervade, that
man will suffer no harm.'

The Rig Veda

ACKNOWLEDGEMENTS

The author would like to thank, John Blackwood, who has collected historical and other material, assisted in the writing of the historical section and reviewed the manuscript.

The author is grateful to Dr James A. Duke of the US Department of Agriculture, Beltsville, Maryland, for his table of biologically active compounds in ginger, and would like to acknowledge his debt to Charles Seely, author of *Ginger Up Your Cookery* (Hutchinson Benham, 1982), for several recipe ideas which have been adapted for this book.

CONTENTS

AUTHOR'S NOTE

This book is intended as an introduction to the wider possibilities of ginger and other medicinal foods. Readers should not take suggestions concerning the use of ginger as prescriptions for specific health problems, but should seek advice and assistance from qualified medical practitioners. The professionals who are most familiar with the use of ginger and other herbs are herbalists, and also naturopaths and practitioners of traditional Chinese medicine and Ayurveda.

CHAPTER 1

Ginger as Medicine

Like all children, those in my family fall prey to the usual childhood ailments. They have had occasional fevers, aches and pains, sore throats, colds, measles, stomach upsets, headaches and so on. This is a natural process, the body's way of learning about disease and how to fight it. But when my children fall ill, we do not go through the automatic reactions of most parents in the modern world. That is, first to be anxious, then call the doctor, then somehow go to him or persuade him to come over, then go through diagnosis, then get a prescription, then go to the chemist and buy the drugs, then give the drugs at the right times, then expect the symptoms to disappear overnight.

Instead, we simply go into the garden to pick herbs, or take down some dried herbs or spices from the kitchen shelves, and make teas and concoctions which we give to the child every once in a while. If it is an infection, we might try a purely fruit diet for a couple of days. We might also use some well tried methods for reducing symptoms, such as wet towels to bring down fever, or a massage with warm olive oil on the chest to reduce a cough at night. We use remedies that have been tested for thousands of years and found to be reliable and safe.

As I am not a medical practitioner, if a health problem looks unusual, serious or mysterious we go to seek advice from a local holistically minded doctor, and ask some pertinent questions. We are particularly interested to know whether the disease is 'self-limiting'—that is, if the body can be expected to throw it off by itself. We ask whether the medical treatment suggested is curative, or only treats the symptoms. Then we go home and

11

normally find that we can digest information and reassurance rather than drugs. Fortunately, over the past 17 years, since we became familiar with natural remedies, we have hardly ever had to take any pharmaceutical drugs. Moreover, when the children do become ill, the disease, such as measles, tends to be mild and over quickly, nor do they suffer the same ailment again and again, as happens so often with problems like stomach upsets, cystitis, bronchial troubles or ear infections.

It might be said that these kids have genetic super-health. This may be true, but is unlikely; after all, they do fall ill. Rather, I am convinced that most children would be strong and well, with an effective immunity, given three basic factors in their life:

1   Natural care, meaning breast-feeding followed by nutritious, wholesome and pure food, clean water and environment, exercise, and a minimum of junk food (such as soft drinks, packaged food and snacks). This is not the subject of this book, but one or two good sources of information are given in the 'Further Reading' section at the end.

2   A secure emotional and physical environment.

3   Safe remedies that work with our natural healing powers when we are ill. Ginger is one such remedy and is the main concern of this book.

At this point you may ask: 'It is all well and good for the experts to treat themselves with these remedies, but can ordinary people also rely on them?'

Of course we can; it is our birthright. The fact is that since the beginning of human history, people have been treating themselves for common ailments with the plants and remedies around them. This information was cultural: it was learnt automatically, just as today we all know how to read the newspaper or switch on the TV. Ordinary people used to learn about hawthorn and horehound in the same way that we now learn about Apple Macintosh and IBM PC.

Today, with most of the herbal lore and knowledge gone, we feel insecure about using herbs when faced with sickness. However, we can gradually relearn these skills and, as we do so, apply them more and more. The degree of success depends on the level of knowledge. The more we know the more confident we shall be about treating simple health problems ourselves with the materials at hand. My purpose in writing a whole book on one herb is to bring this awareness back into circulation, to restore one more item of our lost inheritance, and to provide all of us with one more safe tool for self-care.

It is important to consider to what extent household remedies such as ginger can be used in place of a visit to the doctor. Firstly, we should remember that the doctor never sees most of our passing symptoms. Well known research has shown that three-quarters of all incidents of ill health, such as headaches and tummy aches, are dealt with at home, mostly by doing nothing. So, clearly, if we stock up with a few good herbal weapons and the knowledge of how to use them, we are only gaining.

The second point is that, in all cases, if a disease persists, or if it has dramatic, strong or debilitating symptoms, or if it is racing fast, out of control, or if it is mysterious, of course you should not hesitate to go to your doctor and receive a proper diagnosis. Self-treatment is only relevant in the kinds of mild, non-dangerous family health problems which we discuss in this book, most of which would eventually clear up by themselves anyway.

Thirdly, many of these minor health problems or symptoms may not be curable by the doctor, so we have nothing to lose by trying herbal treatments. For example, influenza is a viral disease which does not respond to any modern medicines, although there are drugs, such as paracetamol, which make the disease more bearable, and natural remedies can do the same.

Fourthly, there is no conflict between professional help and your own self-care. You can do both at the same time. Good doctors will in fact encourage you to assist in looking after yourself during illnesses, so as to be less dependent on medicines and recover more quickly.

Foods and Medicines?

It may seem strange to pop into the kitchen for your medicines rather than the local chemist. This is because it is usually assumed that foods cannot also be medicines, or that even if they have some action on the body, this will be too weak to make a noticeable difference. However, special food components do in fact make the best medicines, because they are so safe. They certainly have effects on the body beyond providing carbohydrates, fats, proteins and vitamins. You have only to consider the sheer dynamite within a teaspoonful of chilli pepper to know how powerful food plants can be.

When we look, for example, at a radish or tomato, we are normally only interested in the food substances it contains. But the plant itself has many more interesting materials waiting to be discovered and used, such as flavourings, aromatics, colours, chemicals that the plant makes to protect itself from insects, or that help it to control its growth, all of which can also have a medicinal, non-nutritional effect on us. At the very least these extra plant substances can prevent disease. One example of this is cancer prevention. It is now well accepted by cancer experts that green, yellow and orange vegetables and fruits can help prevent cancer. It appears to be the minerals, fibre and oily components like beta carotene that are responsible. The National Cancer Institute in the United States is investing twenty million dollars in a 'designer foods' programme to see which protective substances can be added to common staple foods to make them cancer-preventing. These substances are being sought in plants such as garlic, flax seed, citrus fruit extracts, rosemary and liquorice, all of which have both food and medicinal uses.

Again, one of the reasons why we assume that a food is not a medicine is the ignorance within modern society. We learn from childhood that illness is treated by drugs, which have strong and more or less immediate effects on the body. These drugs are pure chemicals sold as little pills. Yet for thousands of years it has been well known that food substances, especially plants like mint, turmeric, garlic, onion, lemon and ginger, are highly effective as medicines, provided that you know how to use them. While living in India, for example, I was struck by the fact that, in many local households, the mother prepared the spice mixtures, and the day's recipes, according to how each member of the family felt, the weather, the season, and any special weaknesses or vulnerabilities within the family. A household member with a vulnerability to arthritic problems would get bitter foods, with hot spices such as chilli, ginger and pepper. However, the food for someone with poor digestion would contain aromatic seeds like aniseed, coriander and fennel, along with mild lentil soups. This is common folk wisdom. The professionals in traditional medicine (such as Ayurveda in India or Oriental medicine in China) have developed this into a science, with elaborate systems for both preventing and treating disease by means of food components.

The Power of Spices

There is a good deal of ignorance about the real power of spices, and indeed why they are used at all. For example, we learned at school that spices were introduced into the diet for the sole purpose of preserving food in hot countries. In medieval times, we were told, they used to put a lot of ground cumin over meat before hanging it, since the poor folk of the time did not enjoy the benefit of refrigeration. This is rather like asking someone who has just emerged from listening to a Beethoven symphony concert, 'Why did you go?' and getting the reply, 'Because it stops the traffic noise!'

The truth is that spices are an amazing discovery; adding them to food achieves a range of very valuable results, of which food preservation is one, but by no means the most important or the most interesting. Here are some of the main uses of spices:

- They offer a concentrated source of valuable nutrients, especially vitamins and minerals. For example, garlic has the highest concentration of selenium of any known food plant, and tamarind has exceedingly high levels of vitamin C.

- They assist in making foods more easily digestible. For example, ginger has been found to contain high levels of the enzymes which break down meat, like those in our stomachs. So ginger acts as a meat tenderiser.

- They help the entire system of the digestion and absorption of foods. Thus the pungent spices such as black pepper and ginger stimulate the circulation in the intestine and aid absorption of the other food components in the meal. Other spices such as aniseed or cumin calm the stomach and aid the digestive process. Many spices help elimination. For example, linseed is a mild laxative, and garlic helps the excretion of fat and cholesterol from the system.

- They can stimulate the appetite, as well as increasing the flow of saliva and digestive juices. For example, fenugreek and nutmeg are appetite stimulants.

- They do indeed act as food preservatives. For example, turmeric and cumin seed will stop food from going off.

- They are also anti-oxidants. For example, rosemary, ginger and bay leaf extracts have been found to be as strong as modern chemical anti-oxidants. They stop rancidity and 'off' flavours.

- They have an important ability to balance the general physiological result of a particular diet. For example, the Indian vegetarian diet can be too 'cooling', allowing too many cold-type diseases such as arthritis or bronchial conditions. The spices warm the diet to create a healthy energetic balance.

- They restore distortions in individual diets. For example, too many beans will cause flatulence, prevented by asafoetida; too much fat will cause obesity and circulatory problems, balanced by onions and garlic; too much starch will cause tiredness or blood sugar imbalances, prevented by fenugreek; and too much fruit can cause mucus, balanced by cardamom.

- They detoxify the body and help to eliminate poisons that may have contaminated the food. For example, cayenne pepper causes poisons to be sweated out, garlic neutralises toxins in the tissues, and turmeric helps to eliminate poisons from the liver.

All these uses are in addition to the specific medicinal use of the spices, by themselves, in the prevention and treatment of disease.

The Renaissance of Medicinal Foods

With such a catalogue of benefits, it would seem worthwhile to add these plants to our diet even if they tasted downright horrible. What a pleasant surprise, then, to find that they add so much to the taste, flavour and aroma of our food. It is like having our cake and eating it too. Or maybe it is not accidental. Perhaps human consciousness is designed in such a way that these beneficial agencies are interpreted as pleasing to the senses. Or perhaps it is the spices themselves which are designed thus, or, most likely, everything is designed together for mutual benefit and interaction. This is certainly something worth mulling over as you cut ginger to rescue your stomach and the room is unexpectedly filled with its full, spicy and exotic aroma.

It is worth remembering that it was not so long ago that these plants were in all the Western pharmacopoeiae (official drug guides). At the beginning of this century, you could find there syrup of ginger, oil of rosemary, dill water, syrup of figs, thyme oil or extract, peppermint oil, and many others. They were replaced by stronger chemical preparations without any testing to see whether the new agents were actually more effective than the old. They were changed simply because they did not fit into the scientific way of thinking. Only now are we recognising that modern medicines carry an unexpected and unacceptable price. They drain both our pockets and our long-term health and well-being.

But times are changing. There is a dramatic renewal of interest in medicinal foods. In 1992, for example, garlic was the fastest-selling Over The Counter (OTC) remedy for the cardiovascular system in Europe, taken in capsules or tablets by five million Europeans every day. In 1991 it was the most popular of all remedies available from chemists in Germany. Today some 300 million doses are consumed annually in the United Kingdom. Others, such as mint, alfalfa, carrot oil, rosemary, cranberry, blackcurrant seed and thyme, are now becoming available in all health outlets. Ginger itself is also taking off as a health supplement, along with other herbs and spices, and it is the purpose of this book to explain how to get the best out of it.

Obvious questions still remain to be answered. When are these spices foods and when are they medicines? How do you take them as medicines compared to consuming them as foods, and are they strong enough when combined in cooking to have real medicinal power?

The answers can never be absolutely cut and dried because these substances belong to both categories simultaneously.

However, you can imagine that if you put a pinch of some ancient dried curry powder which you have had on the shelf into a whole pot of vegetables, and cook them furiously, the minimal spicy constituents will be unlikely to have medicinal effects on your body. Alternatively, if you put three drops of clove oil onto an infected tooth and the pain subsides almost immediately, this can hardly be called a culinary experience. All other cases will be somewhere in between.

In general, if you add spices to food, they will have a mildly preventative effect against disease, the degree depending on how much you put in and how much degradation takes place during cooking. If you put in sufficient to produce a strong taste, you can be sure that most of the physiological effects described in the list on pages 16–17 will occur, especially if you add spices repeatedly to the diet. On the other hand, if you wish to achieve a specific medicinal result, for example the antinausea effects ascribed to ginger in the following chapters, you should take the spice separately from food, in a prescribed quantity. In that way you know you are getting the full dosage. In addition, it is sometimes a sensible precaution to take a medicinal food as a specifically designed medicinal product. This is because, as we shall see in the case of ginger, the food products may be weak, impure and old, and contain a poor amount of the medicinal ingredients. In other words, you can choose either the medicinal or the food aspect of such a plant by selecting the dose and the manner in which you take it.

Why Ginger?

There is more to ginger than meets the eye. Once I had a viral infection and a mid-range fever that seemed to drag on. I was feeling wretched—restless, sleepless, muscles aching deeply, hot inside, constant nausea and an awful headache—the kind of misery that you think will never end when you are in the middle of it, but is soon forgotten when you recover. I asked for a strong ginger tea, made from grated fresh ginger and honey, and the effect was almost instant: I began to pour with sweat. After this, almost everything else sorted itself out. The pains went, my temperature dropped, I could vomit, and I was soon in a deep, healing sleep. The next day I was over it. What happened was that ginger 'resolved' the fever in a manner that was as dramatic as the effects of any modern drug. Only, unlike paracetamol or aspirin, it did not simply take away the symptoms while leaving the disease hanging on to me. It actually precipitated healing and created a fast, natural recovery. It was at that time that I decided to research ginger.

I now realise that ginger is one of the most remarkable of remedies. In the sophisticated world of Chinese medicine it ranks as one of the best. A computerised study of all the constituents of thousands of Oriental remedies, carried out by Professor Brekhman's team from the Far East Science Centre of the former Soviet Union, showed that ginger was the fifth most frequently used of all Oriental remedies. Its role is quite unique—no other herb will substitute. What it does, according to Chinese medicine, is to 'carry' other remedies into the body by aiding their absorption and distribution through the bloodstream and into the organs. The Chinese also use it to unblock channels and wake up tired organs. Science confirms that it opens the blood vessels, creates sweating and warmth, stimulates the heart and thins the blood.

It has some unique effects on the intestines. It is the only herb we know which can prevent motion sickness, and it is the best antinausea remedy. A striking clinical study at St Bartholomew's Hospital in London demonstrated that ginger is more effective than conventional anti-emetic drugs at preventing the very unpleasant nausea and vomiting that often occur when patients wake up from anaesthesia after surgery. It is helpful to our digestive system in other ways, as we shall see later.

Its effects on fevers are also rather special. It is the only remedy that most people can have on hand to treat such a common occurrence as a viral fever. And here we can repeat that for most of these uses of ginger there are no competing remedies, either in modern medicine's armoury or in the herbal medicine chest. Besides being unique, like all medicinal foods it is cheap, easy to prepare, extremely safe, and readily available.

This gives some indication of its value, and more will be revealed in the following chapters. In addition, we shall not forget ginger as part of our heritage, part of our culture, and part of our diet; there is a wealth of interesting information. We shall look at the plant in all its glory, see how it is grown and processed, and examine the source of its aroma, taste and medicinal effects. There are stories galore about its power in traditional village life, especially in India, and tales of a different kind when we come to the spice trade.

Ginger has entered our language. We say that we wish to 'ginger up' somebody or something. The 'Ginger Group' is the name given to a group of Members of Parliament who see it as their task to stir things up a little, and prevent complacency and loss of political values. The word 'ginger' has come into our language to describe a kind of mild, revitalising stimulation. It is somewhere between the full-blown irritation of chilli pepper, and the refreshing arousal of a cold shower or a cup of coffee. Hopefully, by the end of the book the reader will have begun to understand and 'feel' ginger in this and other ways, and it will have become a good friend and ally. Then, once the true nature and possibilities of this one plant are realised, others can follow, to enrich our experience, our health and our lives.

CHAPTER 2

Ginger and the Circulation

Ginger is a warm and pungent remedy. We only have to bite into it, feeling the taste and aromatic warmth spreading through us, to realise that it may be able to warm up, to get moving, some sluggish body processes. This implies it can treat health problems that are associated with cooling down, slowing down, and inactivity. The most important such health problem is heart disease. To know why this is, and to understand whether we really need to stoke our inner fires with ginger, we need to look more closely at our chief health problem, and how it arises from our lifestyle and environment.

What Causes Poor Circulation?

Heart disease is the main cause of death and disability in the modern world. Some two-thirds of the Western population have raised blood cholesterol, and around half will have a heart attack, stroke, or other circulation-based problem written on their death certificate. The source of all this circulatory sickness is not simple to identify precisely, and is caused by many aspects of our lifestyle today. We know, for example, that primitive people in their natural environment do not suffer from such problems, unless they migrate to the towns. Moreover, if we put animals into the kind of environment in which we have put ourselves, they too fall prey to the same kind of heart and circulatory diseases.

We certainly do know, after an immense research effort, that certain factors in our lifestyle increase the risks. Smoking is an obvious one. Another is lack of exercise, and another is an inherited susceptibility to heart attack or raised blood cho-lesterol. Fatty diets and a lot of cholesterol floating about in the circulation act together to increase risk, but this too is not the whole story, for we know that people can eat fatty diets, as they did in our grandfather's day, without being the worse for it. Indeed, evidence from groups like the Bedouin of Israel and Egypt shows that when they live in nature they eat mostly meat but have a low level of heart disease, whereas when they enter cities and civilisation heart disease begins, even though their diet becomes much more vegetarian. From this kind of research, and from looking at personality and behaviour, has arisen the concept that stress greatly increases the risk of such diseases. This 'stress' is ill-defined, but generally means living in a state of too much arousal and general psychological imbalance, a lack of inner peace and well-being.

All this is now well known. But we have to go a little deeper. For all these influences tend to interact with each other. For example, stress raises blood cholesterol as least as much as does a fatty diet. Raised blood cholesterol encourages fatty deposits that fur the arteries. Furred arteries reduce organ function and lead to raised blood pressure, which strains the heart, and so on. More than that, all these influences tend to produce similar internal changes, of which a heart attack is the end result. The arteries become gradually blocked by these fatty deposits, blood flow is restricted, raising blood pressure. The flow of blood and body fluids is reduced to the limbs and surface of the body, leading to coldness, less sweating and less elimination. The tissues get less blood and oxygen, leading to more tiredness and poorer function in many organs of the body, including and especially the heart itself.

We can also look at all the causes for similarities between them. Smoking, for example, harms by constricting the blood vessels, not only in the lungs, but all over the body. Lack of exercise causes the blood vessels to lose their flexibility, like rusty flood-gates, so that they fail to allow sufficient blood through whenever needed. The body becomes underused, the flow stagnates. The same happens with too much food and too much stress. They all lead to congealing in the blood vessels, the circulation becoming closed, crusty and inflexible. Indeed, one of the signs of atherosclerosis (furring of the arteries) is calcium deposits, exactly like those inside a kettle. There cannot be a stronger indication than this of the nature of the problem.

In traditional medicine this whole process is described as a cooling off, or slowing down. Even in modern medicine we talk about circulatory disease as a 'degenerative' disease, or a disease of 'atrophy', meaning wasting away. We talk about the 'hardening of the arteries'. Whereas in modern medicine the problem is looked at descriptively, anatomically, in traditional medicine it is regarded as a process. The hardening is only an end result of a slowing down of the flow of the metabolism, the flow of life energy, which allows junk to be deposited like wastes that settle in a slow-moving stream. And in traditional medicine the treatment is to warm up the system, get it moving again. For example, *garlic* is one classic remedy for the circulation. It is pungent and warming, reduces cholesterol and thins the blood, helping to keep the arteries open. *Gingko biloba* is another, which works by expanding and relaxing the blood vessels on the surface of the body. *Exercise* is now known to be perhaps the best method to get the circulation moving and flexible, to open the vessels, especially the vast net that supplies the muscles and periphery. *Relaxation and meditation* reduce stress in the interior, and relax the entire body along with its vessels. Everyone knows that relaxation warms up the periphery, especially the hands and the feet, as the blood vessels let go their constriction.

Heating from Within: Ginger and Oriental Medicine

Ginger certainly can make you sweat! This is common experience. The warmth that ginger brings to the body is the basis for its action on the circulation. Imagine a hot bath or sauna. The heat spreads through the body, opening the channels, relaxing the tightness in the muscles (including those that constrict the blood vessels), and spreading body fluids evenly throughout the tissues, including those in the outer areas of the body that are most often deprived. This is the kind of action that ginger has, but working from the inside out, rather than from the outside in as in the hot bath.

Cayenne pepper also works this way, and is a constituent of many of the herbalists' professional concoctions for the treatment of circulatory disease. Ginger is rather like cayenne, but milder, less irritating and more suitable for self-treatment as your own kitchen remedy. It is also the preferred warming remedy in Oriental herbalism.

Chinese medicine understands ginger, one of its fundamental remedies, very deeply. It classifies ginger into several types according to the way it is prepared:

Dried Ginger
This is regarded as the most hot, pungent and spicy. It is used to warm the middle of the body and stimulate the *yang ch'i*, that is the basic vitality and body warmth. It disperses blockages in the blood, energy, digestion, metabolism and body fluids. In other words, it really gets things moving! It is used for cold hands and feet, chills, weakness, poor digestion and vomiting, and a weak circulation.

As ginger acts primarily on the stomach, lung and spleen energy paths (meridians), it is very useful in driving out colds, mucus, coughs and bronchial infections, as we shall see in chapter

4. The Chinese use it when the weather or climate is cold and damp, to prevent chills, rheumatic conditions and so on.

For example, one classical Chinese text, the *Shang han lun*, says: 'Thus ginger has a stimulating action on the internal organs, with a warming effect besides. It adjusts the metabolism, eliminates excess fluids that have become stagnant within the body, dispels gas and aids digestion. The remedy is helpful in releasing obstruction and distention beneath the heart [in the digestive system].'

Fresh Ginger

This is spicy, warm and aromatic, and works more on the surface of the body to activate sweating, release toxins, and improve the circulation in the skin and periphery of the body. The Chinese use it especially in fevers and chills, aches and pains, acute rheumatic conditions, coughs, headache and some skin problems. This form of ginger is most like the sauna; you can call it sweat therapy. It is used preventatively when the skin is cold and the circulation is poor and, like dried ginger, sometimes for colds and rheumatic conditions arising from the winter or damp, cold weather.

Roasted or Baked Ginger

This is only relevant to Chinese medicine. It is dried ginger which, after baking, loses its pungency and is bitter and warm. It does not disperse or open the blood vessels and body fluids. Instead it helps the spleen to make and hold the blood in its vessels, quaintly described as 'rallying the blood'. It is used in intestinal bleeding and some other conditions.

In Chinese medicine ginger is never used on its own, but always in combination with other herbs. The Chinese doctor prepares a diagnosis based on bodily signs read with great sensitivity. The surface signs, particularly the pulses, colours and textures of the tongue and skin, tenderness, hot spots and so on, are all an indication of the performance and qualities of the functions inside the body. Remedies are designed to adjust these qualities. For example, a weak and hollow pulse that does not bounce back properly when pressed is actually how hardened and cholesterol-blocked blood vessels feel. Noticing this, a mixture may be prepared that will stimulate the heart, using herbs such as Chinese aconite, Chinese sage (*Salvia milthiorrhiza*), ginger, atractylodes, liquorice, Poria cocos (or Hoelen, a fungus growing on pine roots), Tang kuei (Chinese angelica) and others. The exact mixture will depend on the constitution of the person and the imbalances in various body systems. For example, Tang kuei is used if there is a lack of nutrition and oxygen in the blood, leading to pain on exercising, Poria if there is oedema (waterlogging of the tissues), aconite if the heart requires a boost, and so on. Ginger is an assistant to all these herbs by carrying them— 'conducting' as the Chinese describe it—to the place where they work. It is almost always needed to get the circulation moving.

Scientific Support

As with many herbs, there has been little investment in clinical studies on ginger to see if its classic uses can be confirmed when it is tested on people. However, there has been a number of laboratory studies on animals, and these do confirm the traditional picture described above.

Small amounts of ginger extract, when injected into animals, cause the heart muscles to beat more strongly. Studies at the Pharmacy Department of the Tokushima-Bunri University, Tokushima, in Japan, have demonstrated that the pungent principles of ginger were able to stimulate the atrium (the major heart muscle) to beat with more contractile force. The heart actually beats more slowly, and more strongly. In addition, studies at several other Japanese research centres and universities have confirmed that when ginger extract or its active ingredients are given to animals, their blood pressure is lowered by ten to fifteen points. This is a significant reduction in blood pressure, which stays for some hours.

There is little knowledge to explain how ginger actually achieves this. Very few scientists have been curious enough to investigate where the plant's little molecules end up in the body. One clue was again located by Japanese scientists, this time at the University of Kyoto. They found that pungent molecules from both ginger and cayenne pepper make a beeline for the adrenal glands. There they stimulate the adrenal medulla, the central segment of these hormone-producing glands, to produce its messengers, one of which is adrenalin. Adrenalin stimulates the circulation and warms the body. However, it must be said that this can only be a small part of the picture, as adrenalin does other things that ginger certainly does not do, like stimulating alertness, and constricting the circulation in the stomach and the interior of the body, an effect actually opposite to that of ginger.

What these studies tell us is that ginger opens the blood vessels on the periphery of the body, relaxes the channels and lets more blood through. Because the channels are open, the heart does not have to pump so hard to overcome resistance: it is easier to send the blood coursing along. This lowers the blood pressure. Ginger also seems to gently stimulate the heart, as it contracts more strongly. However, as it does not need to work so hard, the heart rate, or speed of pumping, slows down. In other words, the evidence indicates that, as the Chinese said, ginger spreads the fluids more easily round the body, thus taking the load off the heart, which slows down and reduces blood pressure.

Another helpful property of ginger is that it lowers cholesterol levels in the liver and the blood. Studies by Dr Gujral and colleagues at the University of Baroda, Gujarat, India, have shown that if animals are given a diet which is loaded with cholesterol, such as slabs of butter on a concessionary piece of bread, the cholesterol level in the blood rises dramatically. Ginger is able to prevent much of this rise, provided it is taken over a period of time—it does not work immediately.

Other researchers have confirmed this observation. They have found that as soon as ginger is added to a cholesterol-rich meal eaten by animals, cholesterol is excreted out of the body before it reaches the blood vessels. They suggest that ginger works like a variety of resins from plants and other spices, by removing cholesterol from the body via the liver and digestive system. However, it is not as strong and specific as, for example, garlic.

Ginger and Blood-Clotting

The other side of ginger's ability to free the circulation is its action on blood-clotting factors. This has been intensively studied, especially in Denmark at the Institute of Community Health of the University of Odense. There, Dr Srivastava has been investigating the cell fragments called platelets which are the first stage in the clotting process. These platelets stick to wound edges and initiate clots there, but they also stick to the fur on the inside of narrowed arteries and produce unwanted clots within the system. These can precipitate a heart attack (coronary thrombosis), or stroke. They are extreme cases. But microclots also occur, which further restrict the circulation. People with circulatory problems usually have blood that clots too easily, which is why doctors often prescribe small amounts of aspirin.

Japanese scientists have now produced a patent for an anti-clotting remedy which consists, very simply, of capsules containing 60 milligrams (mg) of one of ginger's main medicinal components, a substance called shogaol.

The Danish team from Odense found that ginger was a very

29

powerful inhibiter of the clumping of platelets, the first stage in the clotting process. It clearly made the blood less sticky. But they were able to go one step further. They were able to look into the mechanism of this process, and found something very interesting—that the platelets were less sticky because they made less *thromboxane* and *prostaglandins*. These are local chemical messengers that have been much researched recently as the agents of pain, inflammation, fever, and other body defence reactions. It is clear that many remedies that treat fever, pain, inflammation, headache and so on work by limiting these local messengers. For example, aspirin itself has a very similar effect, both on the platelets and on the local messengers.

This can help us to understand the way ginger works, and put it in perspective as a remedy. It is known that several spices and medicinal foods can reduce prostaglandins and thromboxane, but they do so in different ways which are too complex to describe here. For example, garlic, like ginger, reduces blood stickiness, but as it does not have the same *kind* of effect on prostaglandins as ginger or cloves, it does not reduce fever and pain as they do. We do not know for sure whether ginger's ability to open the blood vessels and warm the body is also something to do with prostaglandins, but it would come as no surprise if it were. For the expanding and contracting of the blood vessels, and local heating, are among the functions of the prostaglandins and similar kinds of hormones.

Taking Ginger for the Circulation

If we regard ginger as a kind of internal sauna, we shall not go far wrong. Ginger should be taken regularly by those whose circulation needs waking up and warming up. This includes people who:

- Suffer from atherosclerosis and are at risk of heart disease from poor diet, lack of exercise, and so on.

- Smoke heavily.

- Have cold hands and feet.

- Feel cold, with a lack of vitality and energy, especially during cold weather.

- Have 'poor circulation', that is inadequate blood supply to the skin and periphery, manifesting as slow wound healing, and muscle pain on exercise.

As the Chinese state, ginger is only one weapon in a campaign for a return to a healthy circulation. It should be combined with other herbs and treatments. The exact mixture will depend on the individual, and for this reason a sincere attempt to prevent or reduce a circulatory problem would include some professional assistance in designing a herbal and lifestyle regime which is 'personalised' or 'customised'.

Ginger combines very well with other means of improving general health and the circulation. It goes well, in particular, with herbs like hawthorn, mistletoe or lily of the valley, which reduce blood pressure and strengthen the heart, because ginger, unlike these other herbs, spreads body fluids throughout the body. It will help herbs that relax the heart and reduce stress and nervous stimulation, such as polygala (Chinese seneca or milkwort) and zizyphus (jujube or Chinese dates). It also goes well with garlic. Though the two are similar in some ways, both being pungent, lowering cholesterol and reducing blood stickiness, garlic is far more effective at reducing cholesterol and body fat, and dissolving clots. Ginger is more effective at improving circulation around the body and strengthening the heart. Therefore the two accentuate as well as complement each other.

Ginger is obviously an excellent companion to dietary measures. It is particularly useful during a mild fast, or if you are changing your diet. It will help to stimulate energy and circulation at such a time, and will also help to get rid of poisons, create sweating, and clean the body. It is a simple matter to add it to your diet. It is also a useful companion for people embarking on an exercise programme, as it helps sweating and the cleaning out of waste. However, it should not be taken by those who overheat easily, and get very red and sweaty.

People in cold climates can become constricted, in body and sometimes in spirit. If we also suffer from the stress of the modern way of life, our circulation is assailed from both inside and out. Perhaps this is why the problem seems so intractable in countries like Britain, Scandinavia and Germany, while the Italians and French seem to get off very lightly despite an equal dose of unhealthy food, cigarettes and so on. This points to the special value of ginger for those in northern climes. It is clear that we have heeded the message in relation to garlic, which has returned to our lives in a big way. Now it is time to add ginger.

CHAPTER 3

Ginger and the Digestion

The most important and best known use of ginger is on the digestive system. It is the classic medicine for beating nausea, vomiting, poor digestion and indigestion, for protecting against stomach ulcers, and for assisting the absorption of foods and medicines into the body. Before we examine these uses in more detail, we ought to get to know something about our digestion.

Tummy Troubles

Dr Johnson joked, 'He who does not mind his belly will hardly mind anything else.' Yet having an upset stomach is part of daily life for many people. It is regarded as so normal that people look at you in astonishment if you say that you never have such problems. Indeed, to 'belly-ache' has entered our language as a word for grumbling.

The digestion is intimately related to the rest of the body, and to the mind. It can even be said to have a kind of intelligence of its own. If you looked into the belly, you would see there the reflection of passing thoughts in the mind. Where do you feel acute embarrassment, stage fright, or anxiety? Certainly not in the brain where these emotions arise. Why is it that the Japanese word for generosity, largeness of personality, is 'a large belly'? The movements, rumbles, redness, squirts of digestive juices, drips of acid, activity of the millions of little 'fingers' (called villi) that take in fat droplets, a complex telephone network of local and long-distance hormones that control events, even an entire immune system, are all there in the digestion, busily responding to all the

33

changes in the body, in the mind, in the emotions and the environment.

For this reason we can no longer look at the digestive system simply as some kind of flask full of juices, that automatically disintegrates all that comes its way. This 'urn and churn' model is out of date. Consider some common stomach problems. *Indigestion* occurs when the intestine is handed more than it can deal with. But this is a very individual matter, and some people are extremely sensitive to small amounts of certain foods which they find indigestible. Stress and anxiety can cause immediate indigestion. *Wind and colic* are the result of too much of the wrong type of food (such as certain sugars in beans and cow's milk) that is inadequately digested by our own juices. Undigested sugars are available for the intestinal bacteria to work on. They do it their way, and produce a lot of gas and toxins into the bargain.

Nausea and vomiting are normal and common reactions to poisons, alcohol, infections, dizziness, rocking movements, foetal waste products (in pregnancy), and shocks (such as the sight of blood). In all these cases nausea and vomiting are the body's natural attempt to purify itself. *A gastric ulcer* is an open area of self-digestion in the stomach, which is caused by long-term anxiety and stress. It occurs because the constant alarm reaction not only restricts the blood supply to the stomach, but also changes the hormonal environment there. *Allergies* and even some *rheumatic problems* are, according to naturopaths, the result of inadequate digestion letting through into the body harmful and undigested substances. Clearly such problems are mind-body problems.

Traditional medicine, especially Chinese medicine, describes how the environment, the constitution and individual behaviour affect the quality of the digestion. For example, if there is a lack of digestive vital power (*Qi*) due to overwork, there may be abdominal pain and distension, lethargy and signs of indigestion;

there is insufficient power to move the food smartly down the digestive conveyor belt. If cold has invaded the system, even from a change in the weather, there could be abdominal pains, cold hands and feet, and poor digestion leading to a build-up of toxins in the body, headaches, and so on. The proper digestive 'fire' that burns or transforms the food into body energy, power and health, is a key concept of traditional medicine.

Ginger in Ayurvedic Medicine

The most intricate understanding of the process of digestion comes from Indian traditional medicine, Ayurveda. It is a vastly sophisticated system which, like Chinese medicine, has its own theories of life, of matter, and of health and disease. These are part of Indian culture, philosophy and spiritual knowledge. It sees five basic elements as constituting the universe, namely earth, air, fire, water and space. It is said that the West received this teaching from the East via Pythagoras and the early Greeks. These elements are codes for qualities; earth, for example, means the solidity, passivity, or materiality of things. Fire is energy, transformation, heat. Water is the symbol of cohesiveness, attraction and damp. Air implies life, movement and action. Space is the background in which the others exist.

The body is constituted of its own three qualities, or 'humours'—namely *Vata*, corresponding mostly to the air element within ether, *Pitta*, largely the biological fire element located within water, and *Kapha*, the water element with a base in earth. These three humours or *doshas* govern different body types, which then become liable to disease resulting from an imbalance of that *dosha*.

Vata Type
Will tend to be tall, thin, bony, with a dry, cool skin, erratic in

habits, quick of speech, adaptable, indecisive, not inclined to sweat, a light sleeper, nervous, sensitive. He or she will tend to have air-type diseases, including nervous system problems, arthritic and rheumatic complaints and all kinds of pains. A stomach problem, such as diarrhoea, will tend to involve wind, bloating, pain, not much passing of liquids and inadequate digestive function.

Ginger, according to Ayurveda, would be good for Vata-type digestive problems, since it would help absorption and digestive function, warm the intestine and treat the cramps, wind and colicky pains.

Pitta Type
Will tend to be of more medium physique, muscular, with a warm, rosy skin, soft hair, moderate speech, a strong appetite, loose motions, inclined to sweat more, a sound sleeper, critical and prone to anger and argument. Diseases will tend to include inflammation, infections, liver problems, ulcers and skin rashes. Any digestive problem is likely to be more 'fiery—that is, of the diarrhoea type—than digestive problems of the Vata and Kapha types. Diarrhoea in a Pitta type will look like bacterial dysentery. It will be hot, often with fever and thirst, and will involve frequent passing of thin liquid.

Pitta people, fire types, do not get on so well with ginger, and mostly do not need it, because they are already fiery enough. Some of their problems are the result of too much fire. Instead of ginger, a less astringent, soothing remedy for the digestion is recommended, such as coriander, cumin, caraway or fennel.

Kapha Type
Will tend to be heavier, stouter, slower, with a paler complexion, oily hair, thick skin, moderate digestion, tending to have mucus; a person of constant habits, likely to be calm, sentimental, some-

times dull, slow of speech and a heavy sleeper. Diseases may be bronchial and ENT (ear, nose and throat), oedema, mucus problems, swollen glands or growths and stomach problems. In the case of a digestive problem like diarrhoea, there will be heaviness, lethargy and weakness, with passing of much mucus.

Ayurveda tells us that ginger is particularly good for Kapha types, and with Kapha foods. That is, in the diet it helps to absorb and balance watery and oily food, and prevents the heaviness and obesity arising from such foods, especially in a Kapha type of person. It will help to balance overly sweet foods, too much dairy produce, too much to drink, too much fruit and too much meat. Ginger is better at this than pepper or mustard which, though pungent, can be too drying. In general, ginger is good for Kapha types to counteract a tendency to lethargy, congestion and stagnation.

An important concept in Ayurveda is that of *Agni*, or digestive and metabolic fire. If food and other inputs are properly burnt up, processed and digested, they will not create toxins, called *Ama*, which collect in deposits around the body. The furring up of the arteries with cholesterol is a kind of *Ama* deposit, as is arthritic deterioration of the joints.

Ayurveda employs herbs, oils, yoga, massages, dietary principles, colours, gems, minerals and almost anything you can imagine as therapeutic tools. One of the many principles which will help us understand ginger better is that of the six tastes. As in Chinese medicine, herbs are classified by tastes. As in Chinese medicine, herbs are classified by tastes. *Sweet*, for example liquorice, fruit (such as jujube and figs), lovage and angelica, tends to be demulcent, soothing, harmonising, laxative, nutritive, and supporting the body's immunity. *Salty*, for example seaweeds, is softening, mildly sedative, stimulating the digestion in small amounts, and purgative in larger amounts. *Sour*, for example lemon, yoghurt, tamarind and cider vinegar, tends to be stimulating, calming the stomach, relieving thirst and nourishing. *Pungent*, for example ginger, cayenne and garlic, is stimulating and improves body systems, causes sweating, removes extra liquid from the body, and promotes heat, digestion and metabolism. *Bitter*, for example aloe vera, wormwood, feverfew and seneca, is cleansing, detoxifying, reduces inflammation, and stimulates elimination, immunity and secretions. *Astringent*, for example yarrow, raspberry leaf or plantago, stops bleeding, heals wounds, reduces liquids, and prevents diarrhoea.

Ayurvedic medicine considers ginger a pungent herb *par excellence*. It does not have the concentrated irritant pungency of cayenne or chilli, which can sometimes be too strong. Yet it is irritant enough to challenge the muscles and blood vessels and wake them up. It also challenges the internal organs, particularly the digestive system, where ginger is said to awaken the *Agni*, or metabolic fire. Symptoms of low *Agni* include poor digestion, poor absorption, poor circulation, wind, constipation, poor resistance, a tendency to colds and influenza, congestion, body odours and obesity (the latter because there is insufficient fire to balance the water). All of these problems are precisely those which ginger treats.

When *Agni* is improved, it destroys *Ama*. The poisons and undigested wastes are removed. Digestive symptoms such as nausea, which are the result of toxins, are treated, and in the long term, conditions such as atherosclerosis, allergies and rheumatic problems are prevented.

These basic concepts lead to some interesting conclusions about how to use ginger. For example, if we fast, it is good to take ginger tea, especially with lemon, to maintain the metabolic fire. There will be less tiredness, and detoxification will be more complete. If we take a laxative, it can be too strong, causing cramps and wind. By also taking ginger it preserves *Agni*, preventing such symptoms. Indeed, if we take any medicine, it can have a negative effect on our digestion as it passes through it. Ginger will protect the stomach against such damage, which is another reason why it is such a frequent companion within herbal mixtures.

Western Herbalism

Western herbalists have a remarkably similar attitude to ginger, although their language is rather different. They describe ginger as a 'stimulating carminative'. A carminative is a herb that calms and supports the digestion. It soothes the stomach, relieves wind, eases cramps, and generally encourages normal digestion and absorption. The carminative herbs all contain aromatic oils. Examples include the mint family, melissa and verbena (the French after-dinner tisane), caraway, fennel and aniseed (no restaurant in India, even the simplest roadside stall, would fail to give customers some aniseed after a meal), cinnamon, ginger and chamomile.

According to the Western view, these herbs mostly work by relaxing the smooth muscles that make the digestive system work. They also relax the small muscles around the blood vessels of the stomach, bringing more blood to the stomach and improving its function. There is some early European research in which a gastroscope was used to examine the stomach while carminatives were taken. As soon as these herbs entered the stomach, the stomach walls became redder and more folded. This demonstrated that the herbs improved the blood circulation. This, along with relaxed muscles, prevents cramping and pain. Improved circulation gathers up the gases, and speeds up diges-tion. It obviously makes excellent sense to spice our food with these herbs.

In addition there are differences between the various carminatives. For example, the mint family is warming and works well at relaxing the muscles, so it is especially effective against stomach cramps. Chamomile has an additional cleansing antibacterial action so it is effective against upset stomach. The umbelliferous seeds, aniseed, cumin, fennel and caraway, are not so warming but improve the digestion, especially the secretion of digestive juices; they are especially effective against wind and in oiling the wheels of the digestive machinery. Ginger is particularly good at opening the vessels, and stimulating absorption and circulation. For this reason it is classed as a stimulating carminative, unlike fennel, caraway and chamomile, which would be relaxing carminatives.

This fits well not only with the Ayurvedic concepts, but also with the Chinese view of ginger, which similarly describes it as warming to the centre, and improving the digestive fires. In Chinese medicine, ginger is said to *disperse* blockages. If there is congestion of food, blood, fluids, energy, all are stimulated to move along more smartly. Vomiting, nausea, indigestion, gases and stomach pains are seen by Chinese doctors as the result of 'cold' or 'congested' or 'weak' digestive functions. Ginger warms them up, helping them to complete their physiological actions.

Chinese and Ayurvedic medicine would regard a disease such a dysentery as a problem of weak digestive function rather than an infection, as we would view it today in the West. How, they would ask, would the bacteria survive if digestion proceeded apace? Infection can occur only in a stagnant pool, not a free-flowing stream. Consequently, ginger would be included in a mixture to cure bacterial dysentery. In one clinical study, a Chinese hospital in Shandong reported that they used ten grams a day of a paste of raw ginger and brown sugar to treat 50 patients with bacterial dysentery. Seventy per cent were cured in under five days. The rest took a little longer.

Nausea, Vomiting and Motion Sickness

In the autumn of 1985, 80 healthy naval cadets boarded the Danish training ship *Danmark*, a fully rigged but smallish sailing vessel, and sailed off to the rough waters of the Skagerrak. There these inexperienced sailors met a swell of three to four metres and, not surprisingly, two-thirds of them were sick. The ship's doctor handed out pills and assessed the severity of the well-known symptoms—nausea, vertigo, vomiting and cold sweating. The cadets had no notion of what was inside the pills, and they might have been surprised. For 40 of them received pills containing only sugar, namely placebo or 'pretend' pills. The other 40 were given pills containing powdered ginger root. When the results were analysed statistically by Dr Aksel Grøntved of the Svendborg Hospital, the study director, it was found that those taking ginger were much better off. In some cases their symptoms were halved, and the effect lasted for at least four hours.

Dried ginger is not only effective against motion sickness, it appears to be better than the usual drug, dramamine. In a study at Brigham Young University in Provo, Utah, USA, 36 students went through the most uncomfortable process of sitting in a revolving chair that also rose and fell, blindfolded and with their heads to one side. Some were given capsules of dramamine, some of an inert placebo, and the remainder of just under a gram of dried ginger. They did not know which was which, or even what the study was intending to look at. All their symptoms were recorded. None of the group who took the placebo was able to stay in the chair for the full period of six minutes. They were all very sick, and by three minutes their symptoms were rated at around 900. The dramamine group were able to stay a little longer: by four minutes their symptoms were up to a score of around 550, but they too could not stay until the end. Only those in the ginger group lasted the course, and by six minutes their symptom score was only about 200.

This kind of study has been repeated several times, and has put ginger before the public eye as the only serious natural remedy for motion sickness. It is well known that the conventional drugs against motion sickness, such as dramamine, work on the nervous centres in the brain that cause the upset, and may therefore induce drowsiness and lethargy. So they cannot be used by car drivers, seamen, astronauts and those very people who need them the most. For this reason ginger was quickly taken up by NASA for testing for possible use by space shuttle crews. Unfortunately they found ginger to be apparently ineffective against motion sickness. We do not know the reason for this scientific conflict, and at this stage there are insufficient details published on these studies to hazard a guess.

Ginger is widely used in the East against travel sickness. More than one traveller from China has recounted how the buses seem to reek of it as people chew their way through small pieces from time to time. In fact a dose of one gram of dried ginger is best, taken at least half-an-hour before travelling.

Nausea and vomiting can have a variety of causes. Are there cases where ginger should not be used? Occasionally it is better to encourage vomiting rather than suppress it. If poisons or bad food produce the nausea, vomiting can be stimulated by the herb lobelia or by a teaspoonful of salt in a glass of water. In some cases where nausea has a nervous origin, herbal treatment should be accompanied by relaxation, warming the body and sleep, and perhaps here mint or chamomile tea would be better than ginger. Where there is hyperacidity, gastric ulcers and indigestion, both Indian and Western medicine prefer to use aromatic bitter herbs to stimulate the secretion of digestive fluids, rather than ginger. These herbs include gentian, aloe vera, marshmallow, boldo (a Chilean evergreen shrub) and angelica.

Morning Sickness and Drug Side-Effects

Otherwise, ginger is very widely useful since it acts as an energising balm to the stomach itself, rather than on the brain centres as do modern drugs, so that the precise cause of the sickness is not so relevant. For example, ginger as tea, or in capsules or tablets, is perhaps the most effective remedy for morning sickness during pregnancy. A recent clinical trial involving 30 women with the most severe kind of morning sickness, termed 'hyperemesis gravidarum', was reported in the *European Journal of Obstetrics and Gynaecology*. It showed that one gram of powdered ginger per day greatly reduced the symptoms, and in some case eliminated them.

Remember, however, that in pregnancy the fewer remedies that are taken the better. Large amounts of spices rank as medicines and therefore during this time should not be taken unnecessarily. Avoid excessive doses. It is also worth remembering that morning sickness is not an inevitable and necessary curse. It is the result of some imbalances within the system, which allow accumulation of toxins from the foetus. The body becomes overloaded with waste products and tries to remove them by vomiting. Natural therapists and herbalists will often recommend nutritional support to improve the condition of the blood. For example, alfalfa, nettle, oats, kelp, pollen, spirulina (a nutritive alga) and B complex can be of help.

Nausea and vomiting may also occur as a side-effect of drugs, poisons, anaesthetics or almost any toxins in the body. Ginger is highly effective in such cases. This is well illustrated in the remarkable study mentioned in chapter 1, in which 60 patients at St Bartholomew's Hospital were given ginger against post-operative nausea and vomiting. These side-effects are caused by the anaesthetics, and they are particularly unpleasant and difficult to deal with. Doctors are obviously reluctant to give further drugs that cause drowsiness at this time. Only half a gram of ginger was given before the operation to one group of women who were undergoing major gynaecological surgery. For comparison, another group were given 10 mg of metoclopramide, a conventional antinausea drug. A third group received an inert 'pretend' pill or placebo. Those taking ginger had much less nausea and vomiting than the others. None of the women taking ginger needed any anti-vomiting drugs after the operation, in contrast to those in the other groups. The authors, Dr Bone and colleagues, point out that 'there has been no real reduction during the last 50 years in [post-operative nausea and vomiting] which remains at 30%, despite the continued introduction of new anti-emetics . . . Ginger has the major advantage over other substances in that it does not have any recorded side-effects.'

Not surprisingly India, which has an indigenous medical system still intact, has thought of this before. A special ginger-containing remedy called Gasex is used in some hospitals after surgery to prevent nausea, wind and other intestinal discomforts. Tests show it to be highly effective.

One very distressing consequence of taking anti-cancer drugs is the nausea and vomiting that are the usual side-effects. Ginger will help to reduce these symptoms. This is supported by some preliminary research. A clinical study of the use of ginger against nausea from chemotherapy has just begun at St Bartholomew's Hospital in London.

Clearing Out Poisons

We mentioned that according to Ayurveda, ginger increases *Agni*, the energy of transforming nutritive substances, and in so doing reduces and destroys toxins. In fact, if we think about the way ginger opens the blood vessels, spreads fluids properly throughout the body, stimulates the flow of bile (waste products from the liver) and causes sweating, it is logical that it also helps to remove poisons and toxins. The more the toxins sit around in one place, the more harm they do. This is another case where we can apply the well-worn image of the stagnant pool.

In traditional Chinese medicine, removing toxins is one of the major uses of ginger. It is given as an antidote to poisoning from food, from drugs, and from other herbs. In other words, it was added to herbal mixtures as an antidote to their toxic ingredients. This was recognised by physicians and herbalists in the West, too. Peter Holmes reminds us of this in his classic text, *The Energetics of Western Herbs*, which has an excellent review of the true nature, properties and uses of hundreds of herbs. He quotes Henry Barham (1794) who states that ginger is 'a corrective of many medicines . . . [which] taketh away their malice'.

In modern China ginger juice is used as an emergency remedy for poisoning: 5ml of the juice is taken as a gargle and then swallowed, and another teaspoonful given every four hours. Presumably it causes a great deal of sweating, heat and stimulation, and will be especially good against those poisons which depress the body. In modern medicine they also give stimulants and even a slap in the face in such cases.

Restoring the Digestion

In chapter 1 I gave a list of sound reasons why spices should be added to our food on a regular basis. Some of these reasons related to the assistance that these spices give to our digestive system. Drawing largely from the Ayurvedic knowledge, we shall look briefly at some other digestive problems.

Diarrhoea can have many causes, such as dysentery, bad food, nerves, virus or parasite infections. As we have seen, apart from the Pitta types, ginger is used to help create absorption in the intestine, together with other spices such as cardamom and coriander, and a bland whole-grain diet. In addition, astringent herbs such as bilberry, cranesbill, tormentilla (bloodroot) or garlic may be used to stop infection and dry inflammatory secretions. Diarrhoea can be of several types according to the Indian classification. The Vata type can have more pain, wind, cramps, and not much liquid, while Kapha-type diarrhoea tends to be cool with more mucus. The above treatment is suitable for both. The Pitta type, however, which is more of a watery, hot, inflammatory diarrhoea, should not be treated with warming spices. Bitters such as gentian, wormword or golden seal can be used, especially for the Pitta type.

Constipation is the mirror image of diarrhoea, and it too can be the result of many factors, particularly a long-term diet with insufficient roughage and vegetables, insufficient physical activity, anxiety, overstimulation and overwork, medical drugs, and other factors which slow down the normal rhythms of the digestive system that shunt the food down its long, winding path. Again, constipation generates toxins, which may cause long-term health problems, including rheumatic problems, liver problems, nervous conditions such as chronic headaches, and low immunity. This is now so well known that even a normal family doctor will question you about your bowel movements in investigating chronic diseases.

Generally, constipation is treated by a change in diet, which should normally begin with a fast, taking little except fruit or vegetable juices. Enemas, sweating therapy and other detoxification procedures are helpful. After this, a diet with plenty of roughage, such as oatmeal, bran and salad vegetables, as well as yoghurt, whole grains, prunes, nuts, and cold pressed oils, will often correct the problem. A Vata-type constipation is typically caused by lack of moisture in the digestive system. There will be wind, bloating, pain and headache, and the constipation may be harder to get rid of. Bulk laxatives such as psyllium or linseed are useful here. Castor oil or olive oil may also be effective. If persistent, stronger laxatives such as rhubarb or senna should be used. In all cases ginger and other spices are very useful to keep the digestion moving, and also to balance the laxatives.

In the Kapha, water type of constipation, the digestion will tend to be congested, with much mucus or phlegm, which may also produce problems in the chest and throat. The person will feel lethargic and heavy, and be overweight. In this case bulk laxatives, such as linseed, should not be used as they increase the mucus. The bitter laxatives such as aloes and senna are effective, along with fasting and a lot of exercise. Again, ginger and hot, stimulating herbs such as pepper are effective. Finally the Pitta or hot type of constipation is often accompanied by fever, or the result of fever, and may cause feelings of thirst, irritability, sweating, distention and pain. In this case one should drink a lot, eat a light, cooling, raw food diet, and take mild, bitter laxatives such as cascara, aloes or yellow dock. Ginger or hot spices are not recommended.

Ginger and Absorption

In the early part of this century it was fashionable to look on many health problems as the result of a disturbance of the normal intestinal flora, the rich culture of helpful bacteria that inhabit our intestine. At that time it was assumed that the spices help us by being antibacterial, by stopping invasions of the wrong bacteria. We now know that although this is correct, that the essential oils within the spices are antibacterial as well as anti-oxidant and food preserving, it is only a very small part of the picture. Thus, in the case of ginger, laboratory studies have indeed demonstrated that it greatly inhibits the bacteria in the colon that work away at any undigested sugars (for example, from hard-to-digest beans), creating gases. But at the same time it is now known that a more important action is to create more complete digestion and absorption of foods, farther up in the digestive channel. This is more helpful in preventing wind and digestive upsets than the antibacterial action lower down.

The scientific work exploring ginger's assistance to normal digestion is still very incomplete. There is some evidence that ginger, along with other spices, promotes the secretion of digestive fluid. We have already mentioned that it can be seen to bring blood to the stomach walls, and that it has been proved to be what is known as a cholagogue—that is, it stimulates the flow of bile, which is certainly an advantage in the digestion of fats and the elimination of waste. But, again, these are studies on animals, and need to be confirmed by some clinical work before ginger can be expected to make its way back into the pharmacopoeias.

One of the main reasons why ginger is added to so many mixtures or prescriptions in Chinese or Indian traditional medicine is that it helps absorption of the other constituents. Ginger is often described as the messenger or servant that brings other medicines to the site at which they should act. There is in fact some preliminary scientific evidence from India that ginger can increase the absorption of pharmaceutical drugs, and also protect the stomach from damage by aspirin and other similar non-steroid anti-inflammatory drugs.

This is a potentially fascinating use of ginger, namely that it is useful not only to normalise the digestion, but also to help with the absorption of drugs, herbs, vitamins and nutritional components. It would mean that we could reduce the dosage of drugs, or make them work more efficiently, and therefore more safely. It would mean better nutrition if we combined our soups or our supplements with a little ginger, and it would mean that our much abused intestines would have a little protection from all the medicines and other substances they have to cope with.

Ginger itself is absorbed extremely fast. Research has shown that its pungent powerhouse molecules can race into the body. In one second they are across the stomach wall. No wonder that they open the way to other substances to follow.

As we shall see in chapter 7, the most famous folk rhyme on ginger seems very true: 'Run, run, as fast as you can, you can't catch me, I'm the gingerbread man!'

CHAPTER 4

Ginger for Coughs, Colds, Aches and Pains

It is said that King Henry VIII discovered that ginger was good against the plague, and recommended it to his loyal subjects. Consequently everyone began to eat gingerbread, baked in the shape of little men with round bellies. Whether this was to please the king or tease the king, or a leftover of an ancient pagan rite, is anyone's guess. But this is the legendary origin of the gingerbread man.

At that time, with the plague threatening, eating ginger must have been rather like clutching at straws. For we know that ginger is not an antibiotic. But it does have another very useful function during colds, flu, virus infections, coughs, chronic bronchial problems and low grade infections of all kinds. As we have shown, it can warm the body, improve the circulation and activate the body's defences. This has even been noticed by modern medicine, at least until recently, for ginger was described in the pharmacopoeias as a cough and cold remedy, as well as a carminative and a flavouring agent.

Ginger does not specifically attack the virus or bacteria. Nor is it an expectorant, that is a medicine that loosens mucous secretions allowing a cough to get them out. Instead it brings in body fluids to the area, warming it up. This mobilises the body's defences, encouraging them to take the situation a little more seriously and not be so complacent and lethargic. Thus, in the case of a cough, there is more secretion so the phlegm is thinner and can be coughed up; there is more sweating, driving out the toxins and the virus; there is more immunity, more white cells, and above all, a better circulation to spread this immune system into all those hard-to-reach places. Mustard plaster used to be an old-fashioned folk remedy for bronchial problems. It is also heating and pungent, working in much the same way as ginger.

Clearing Colds

Colds, chills, coughs, bronchitis, flu and catarrh are all signs of what the Chinese would call 'invading cold' and/or 'invading damp'. Cold and damp have got in to the system from the climate or environment, and have to be driven out with warm, pungent remedies that encourage sweating. In these cases, Chinese medicine would add one more description—that they are 'exterior' conditions, disturbances of the outer areas of the body, not in its deep centre among the organs. In such cases we want ginger to work more on the exterior, producing sweating and improving the peripheral circulation. As we saw in chapter 2, fresh ginger is better at warming the exterior and causing sweating, while dry ginger is better at warming the interior, and does not cause so much sweating.

There are many choices in the treatment of colds. In the early stages, drink ginger tea with lemon and cloves, or take ginger tablets. Vitamin C has proved very helpful in nipping viral diseases, including colds, in the bud and greatly reducing their severity. Eat very lightly or not at all, with no oils, fats or dairy products, all of which increase mucus and congestion (increasing Kapha, or phlegm). Once the cold is established the focus is as much on clearing mucus and congestion as it is on warming. Now add inhalations of mentholated balm (a little balm in a bowl with added hot water) and sage tea. You can also put a tiny amount of balm on the nostril entrance to clear the congestion, and massage it onto the forehead or temples if there is headache or sinus problems. Sage is a very effective herb for drying secretions, and it is our standby in such cases. Garlic and onions with honey is another helpful mixture. Keep taking ginger throughout to continue sweating out the cold and to ensure that the inner warmth drives it away. It can make the difference between a cold that seems to drag on and on and one that takes its natural course and is quickly overcome. Other herbs useful in colds are elderflower, lemon balm and catnip teas. They all warm up the body gently, and help relieve bronchial problems.

In the case of coughs, the classic herbs are horehound, elecampane root (scabwort) and coltsfoot. They will reduce the secretions and soothe the area. They can be added to the cold treatments if the cough arrives on top of the cold. If these herbs are combined with liquorice and ginger, their effectiveness is increased because their power is spread better throughout the lungs, chest and body.

Ginger in Fevers

In the case of influenza, or viral fevers in general, it is important to know how to use ginger. It should be taken at the stage of the fever where there is shivering or cold hands and feet, and a sensation of chill. It can help the uncomfortable, restless, low grade fever which doesn't 'break' and appears to be dragging on. In such cases fresh ginger, grated into a drink with honey and lemon, may help to bring out the fever. That means, to bring the heat out from the centre to the periphery, to warm the hands and feet, to create sweating and to hasten the 'crisis' as it used to be called—that is, the break-point where sweating is profuse, the fever suddenly drops, and you feel much better. It should not be used, however, if the fever is high, you feel hot, you are red and sweating, and you need to bring down the temperature.

This is the way to use ginger to hasten natural healing. It is the opposite path from using drugs such as paracetamol to suppress the fever, allowing the disease to linger without a full cure.

Fever is not something to fear. It is the body's own defence reaction, for the high temperature not only mobilises the immunity, but is decidedly inhibiting to the multiplication of viruses. The head is the part of the body most sensitive to fever, so it can be controlled by applying cool wet towels, or sponging the body with tepid water.

Japanese researchers have shown that ginger can reduce coughing in animals, though they used high and unrepresentative doses. A thorough study of ginger's actions in fever has been carried out by Dr N. Mascolo of the University of Naples together with colleagues at the University of Rajasthan in India. They found that ginger was able to lower temperature in animals which had fever, but did not affect their temperatures when normal. It was nearly as effective as aspirin. They suggested that ginger worked somewhat like aspirin, by reducing the production of prostaglandins, a fact we have already discussed in chapter 2. Of course ginger is not the same as aspirin, and these studies are a great oversimplification, but they are a beginning.

Rheumatic Problems

The stiffness, slowness and pain that result from rheumatic conditions, as we saw in chapter 2, are all regarded in Chinese medicine as the result of the entry of cold and damp into the body, something well known to all rheumatism sufferers who are very sensitive to the weather. The whole process of the joints losing their lubrication, function and warmth is seen as cooling or, as we would say it in the West, atrophy. Ginger is one of the classic remedies for these conditions, used both internally and externally. Since the heat is needed near the surface of the body, fresh ginger is used in treatment. However, dried ginger is used as a general preventative of such cold conditions.

In China, fresh ginger teas are drunk in all such cases, or ginger is mixed with other medicines. It is also injected by doctors at the site of the rheumatic joint, or on nearby acupuncture points. Ginger poultices are another method of administration. A clinical trial at the Guangdong Province Research Centre into Medicinal Plants tested the injection method with 113 patients with rheumatic problems or chronic backache. A small amount was injected every other day into the region around the rheumatic joint. There were some burning sensations, numbness or pain, which soon went. The method resulted in considerable improvements in the pain, swelling and stiffness in more than 90 per cent of the rheumatic patients. It was less effective in those with backache. Thirty-eight of the patients had rheumatoid arthritis and of these 14 were cured, a considerable improvement was obtained in a further 14, and six more showed some improvement. The remaining four were not helped.

Of course, you would be unlikely to want to inject fresh ginger into your joints, and in any case it should only be done by a qualified practitioner. You may achieve a significant improvement if you take enough by mouth. A report in the journal *Medical Hypothesis*, written by Dr Srivastava whom we previously met on p. 29, describes seven patients with rheumatoid arthritis who were all greatly improved by taking fresh ginger. The average dose was about one ounce daily.

The treatment of rheumatic conditions is not simple and one-track, whether through herbs, homeopathy or conventional medicine. Many remedies are potentially useful depending on the person, the nature of the rheumatic problem and the stage of the disease. In Indian medicine, rheumatic problems are seen as the result of toxic accumulations, or *Ama*. Treatments are designed to clear these toxins from the body; these include mild laxatives and liver-strengthening remedies, the liver being the great house-cleaner of the body. Ginger, galangal and other spices are used to increase *Agni* or fire, to burn up toxic accumulations. Turmeric is also used because it has additional anti-inflammatory properties.

There are other specific herbs to treat the bones and joints, improve flexibility and lubrication. One of the most important in Ayurvedic medicine is called guggul, known to us as *Commiphora mukul*, a resinous plant and a relative of myrrh. The plant is boiled with other herbs to make a compound herbal resinous tablet, which is commonly used in Ayurveda for treatment of arthritic and rheumatic problems, along with other conditions such as atherosclerosis.

In Western herbalism the same principles are used for cleaning out the body by both regulating the digestion and recharging the liver. Herbs such as dandelion root and burdock are used for this purpose. As in Ayurveda, herbs such as celery seed, parsley seed and juniper are used to remove deposits from the body and increase circulation and urination. Devil's claw, yucca, nettle, black cohosh (an American root, known also as bugbane) and meadowsweet are a few of the herbs used to treat the condition itself. They are often combined with cayenne or ginger.

Menstrual Problems

Almost any health problem that involves stagnant energy, and especially stagnant fluids in the body, will be helped by ginger. It is especially appropriate where the congested, clogged liquids do not constitute an acute serious health problem but cause a general lowering of health.

Menstrual problems are such an instance. Menstruation is a good indicator of general health, because any disruption of normal balanced flows of energy and fluids will show up there. Menstruation can be regular, without pains, discomfort, cramps, tension, headaches or emotional storms. Or, as is very often the case, it can be scanty, irregular, excessive, late and accompanied by a range of symptoms loosely lumped together under the title PMT. These may include tension, emotional upsets, swollen breasts, tiredness and irritability and all the symptoms described above.

The causes may well be the same as those that disrupt bodily harmony in other systems, such as that of the digestion: over-work, stress and anxiety, too much fat, sugar and starch in the diet, with too few minerals and vitamins. Degraded purified oils and animal fats are particularly suspect.

Ginger, turmeric, basil and vervain (verbena) are used as mild remedies for what the Chinese would call 'stuck' or 'stagnant' blood. They are all effective in moving the blood to create regular, easy menstruation. And they are mild. Tang quei (Chinese angelica) is the main Chinese herb in this category, and it is widely used by Oriental women and increasingly by women in the West. Stronger Western herbs also exist, such as rue, pennyroyal and motherwort, but they should not be used indiscriminately, and preferably with professional guidance.

Again, take your constitution into account. For example, menstrual problems that are 'watery' in nature (that is Kapha type) include swollen breasts, oedema, heaviness, tiredness, crying and mucous discharges; against a background of a Kapha constitution (tending to obesity) they can be successfully treated with pungent spices like ginger. The Vata type will be irregular and scanty, with mood swings, instability, anxiety, pains and headaches. Gentle spicy remedies, such as aromatic herbs, cham-omile, mint, Chinese angelica, dill, turmeric, liquorice and a little ginger, will work here. For the fire (Pitta) type problem, involving sweating, heat and hot flushes, rashes, abundant flow, anger and so on, more cooling emmenagogues (blood-moving) herbs are required, such as skullcap, yarrow, motherwort, calendula and dandelion.

CHAPTER 5

Ginger: Cultivation and Commerce

You may never have seen fresh ginger. Although it is becoming more common in our supermarkets, to many of you ginger may be little more than some brownish-yellow powder, smelling of dust and pungency, in a plastic bottle that has been sitting in the kitchen spice rack since time immemorial.

Fresh ginger is an extraordinary sight. It is fleshy and bulbous and looks rather like several small potatoes clumped together and then flattened. The main segments are about 80 cm long, 40 cm wide and 15 cm thick. They bear fat branches about 20 cm long on the upper side, giving the whole the appearance of a hand with blunt, stubby fingers. Indeed the technical term in the spice trade is a 'hand' for the whole, and 'fingers' for the branches. It has a smooth, corky skin, buff or creamy brown, covering white and juicy flesh.

The Ginger Plant

Botanically speaking, fresh ginger is not a root. It is in fact an underground stem, known as a rhizome, which bears buds on the top of each of its stubby fingers, and grows a mass of thin, tangled roots below. These roots are scraped off before the ginger arrives in the shops so we do not see them, and often make the mistake of thinking that the rhizome is itself a root.

Under suitable conditions of dampness and temperature, the buds sprout. First appears a rolled-up green tube, which then opens out as a stem, or more accurately a 'pseudo-stem', because the ginger hand itself is the underground stem. The above ground pseudo-stem can be a metre tall, and bears blade-shaped leaves that branch out ladder-like on either side (see cover drawing).

Ginger does not usually flower, but when it does it produces an exceptionally beautiful cluster of white or yellow flowers, flecked with purple, each held in a small green cup. The whole cluster appears on its own long spiky stem, somewhat like a gladiolus.

Fresh ginger, when cut, produces a typically warm, spicy, refreshing aroma. It has a pungent, aromatic, lemony, and slightly bitter taste. Dried ginger is less fresh and lemony, and rather more warm, woody and pungent. This dried ginger is a shrivelled version of the 'hands' of the fresh ginger. Its pieces are hard, small and flattened, having lost 80 per cent of their weight and size in the drying process.

The Ginger Family

Ginger is given the botanical name *Zingiber officinale* Roscoe. Ginger belongs to the family Zingiberaceae, along with many hundreds of different plants, some of them quite important to man. First there are the plants which are very close to ginger botanically—that is, different types of gingers, belonging not only to the family Zingiberaceae, but also to the Zingiber group within it. There is *Zingiber cassumunar*, known in India as forest ginger. It is used widely in Indian medicine against diarrhoea and colic, and as a substitute for real ginger. In Thailand it is used very widely as a flavouring spice, with an odour and taste like that of ginger but more camphoraceous and musty. The plant looks very like true ginger, with a similar rhizome which has a rich yellow interior. In Thailand the plant is known as *phlai*, which may have led to jokes about *Thai Phlai*.

Another type of ginger, *Zingiber zerumbet*, is widely cultivated throughout Asia, mostly as a medicine for coughs, asthma, stomach aches and colic and, unlike true ginger, seems to be very popular for skin diseases. It tastes and smells like a bitter version of ginger, but its underground parts, its rhizome and roots, are gigantic. *Zingiber mioga* is the Japanese ginger, grown and used there instead of real ginger. However, it is so similar that no one in the spice trade bothers to differentiate it botanically from ginger grown in India or elsewhere. So it is usually lumped together with the official ginger. Its flavour is much fruitier, more like bergamot. *Zingiber elatum* and *Zingiber chrysanthum* are other species of very aromatic Asian gingers.

A little farther away, not a brother but a cousin of ginger, is turmeric, *Curcuma longa* L. It looks rather similar as a plant, and indeed, if you saw the dried rhizome you might think it was ginger. However, it is far less aromatic, and has a deep yellow colour, orange when fresh. Turmeric is an exceedingly important Indian spice and medicine. It really deserves a book on its own. One of its key uses in India is as an antibacterial skin treatment. A paste of turmeric is placed on any skin infection or eczema. It will draw out boils and ulcers, and is generally the first aid remedy in traditional Indian households for minor cuts and wounds. At every little Indian roadside stall you will find turmeric soap, scented with sandalwood, which is the cheapest and most popular available. It seems infinitely preferable to today's synthetic white supermarket soaps, and it is about a tenth of the price. Turmeric's antiseptic properties are also useful in food. It stops food going off, and will help to treat stomach infections due to bad food or water.

The main active ingredient of turmeric is a yellow compound called curcumin, although there are certainly others. This compound, along with turmeric itself, has been found to be strongly anti-inflammatory. It makes turmeric one of the best anti-inflammatory herbs known, a gentle herbal rival to cortisone. It is used internally for injuries, to promote liver function and dissolve gallstones, and in dysmenorrhoea and inflammations of the urogenital system. In many ways it is a non-pungent version of ginger, for it seems to act similarly on the prostaglandins but not to have ginger's warming properties.

Another well-known relative is cardamom, *Elettaria carda-momum* Maton. The leaves look rather similar to turmeric—long ovals with prominent ribs running along them—but in this case it is the seed that is eaten as a spice. It certainly does have a very special and exquisite aroma, and it used to be called the 'queen of spices'. Cardamom is also used as a medicine, and is extremely popular in the West as an essential oil. It is gently warming, removing wind and indigestion, and reducing mucus in the stomach and the lungs.

There are several cheaper substitutes for the classic cardamom. They belong to the *Amomum* species, and are not usually found in Western shops. For example, there is the wonderfully named 'grains of paradise' (*A. melegueta*), and there are *A. subulatum* and *A. aromaticum*, which are usually known simply as 'large cardamom' or sometimes simply amomum. They are spicy and have a cardamom-like aroma, although the aroma is a little rougher.

The ginger family also includes a number of plants which are more medicinal than culinary, although used for both purposes. For example there is galangal—actually two plants, greater galangal (*Alpinia galanga*) and lesser galangal (*Alpinia officinarum*). It may be more familiar to some as 'china root'. Galangal is somewhat like ginger root when dried, but reddish and rounded. It has a sweet, aromatic smell. It has been well known and used in Europe for over a thousand years, presumably brought by the Arabs who introduced many herbs to Europe. It is still used in India, the Baltic states and the Middle East in making aromatic herb teas and beers. In the Galilee hills, where I now live, the Druze and Arabs will traditionally give a tea heavily spiced with galangal to women after childbirth. I have been presented with galangal tea several times when attending celebrations for the birth of a child. Medicinally it has very similar uses to ginger.

Zedoary (*Curcuma zeodaria*) is similar to turmeric, grey in colour, with a bitter but aromatic taste, and used as a stomach remedy. Since the Middle Ages it has been a constituent of a number of bitters that have stimulated jaded appetites and treated dyspeptic European tummies.

How To Grow Ginger

Those of you braving the winter winds in Britain and Northern Europe will have to make do with your local greengrocer for a supply of fresh ginger to keep you warm. For ginger is a hot weather crop, growing in countries like India, Australia, Jamaica, China, and Nigeria. It cannot abide frost. However my colleague, John Blackwood, has grown ginger very successfully indoors in southern England, so glasshouses or conservatories that never get too cold would suffice.

The plant does not like too much heat either, and will not grow in the hottest tropical areas, or in dry heat or desert conditions. It does best when the climate is hot and moist and it can find a little shade from the direct glare of the noonday sun. It also likes to be in moist soil. Mulching is very helpful to stop the top layers of the soil drying out and damaging the sensitive roots near the surface. That is why, as a rain-fed crop, it is planted at the beginning of the monsoon in India. In other places it is irrigated well.

You can plant it in spring. Take a ginger 'hand' and split it into half-ounce (15 g) pieces, each with one good fat bud on it. Plant them in a raised bed or mound, about four to six inches (10-15 cm) in the soil, and spaced ten inches (25 cm) apart. The earth should be loose and rich with plenty of organic material and rich compost. Ginger feeds heavily, exhausting the soil of its nitrogen, potash and minerals. Put a good mulch over the ground after planting and renew it where necessary. Soon after planting you will see the long spiky leaves appearing and unrolling more or less in front of your eyes.

After six months it can be harvested. Some very interesting research has been carried out on the right time to harvest ginger. It matures in the soil rather like a carrot or a radish, becoming stronger in flavour and more fibrous as time goes on. If it is harvested early it yields a succulent, tender ginger, aromatic, lemony and mildly flavoured. This is the tender 'green' ginger which is harvested commercially for sale as fresh ginger, or for making ginger sugar syrups. If one waits for a couple more months, the flavour becomes stronger as more of the pungent components build up in the flesh. It is then a little drier and more fibrous. Commercially it is harvested at this time for drying and selling as the full-flavoured and pungent dried whole ginger. The latest harvest, at around nine months, is strongest of all, richest in pungent components, and quite dry. This is used commercially for drying and then grinding as powdered ginger.

There are some diseases that attack ginger, although these are more of a problem in intensive agriculture than with pots in the conservatory. Like many root crops, it is susceptible to fungi that cause root rot, in which the ginger rhizome becomes soft and rotten. There is little to be done in such cases other than to dig up the affected plants and burn them. It is best to protect against this by using the cleanest possible ginger for seed, and washing it with fungicide before planting. Yellowing of the leaf may occur, as with potatoes or tomatoes, and again this is a fungal problem which can be treated with Bordeaux mixture.

If we took a journey to the south-west of India, to the rich, gently sloping farmland of Kerala state, and went to visit a ginger farm, what would we see? We might see several small fields of an acre or so. They would be growing tapioca and chillies, lines of little green bushes flecked with scarlet pods, or sesame, tall and stout with an exquisite purple flower. One of the fields would have many raised beds of a metre width, surrounded by narrow drainage channels. The soil would be very richly manured, dark and friable. In March of April you might see the farmer, dark skinned and wearing a coloured *lungi* (short wrap-round cloth), and his wife and family, dressed in bright and spotlessly clean saris, digging holes and planting the pieces of ginger a hands-breadth apart. Soon after planting the field would have a dressing of fertiliser, and then you would see the children spreading a mulch of green leaves all over the beds, to keep in the moisture and prevent the soil being washed away by heavy rains. At occasional intervals after that, on dry days, all the family would be out, weeding the beds by hand, or earthing up the tall, spiky ginger plants with a hoe. Come December, you would see the field take a yellow hue, as the tops began to dry up. The farmer would be out again with his family, carefully lifting the clumps with a spade and putting them in baskets, which the women would carry off to the shed for washing.

If you can provide the right conditions, ginger is not so difficult to grow, and it is well worth it, especially if fresh ginger is hard to get in your area. I enjoy growing it, watching the spiky leaves unfurl day by day, and thinking of those heady flavours maturing under the earth. Here in Israel, in our Mediterranean climate, it does well—if we can stop the cats from digging it up first.

Ginger in Commerce

On a recent visit to India I travelled up the famed Malabar coast, passing through towns whose names were made famous by the spice trade: Quilon, Allepey, Calicut and Cochin. In the last of these, wandering through the small streets, I was jostled by the ceaseless hurrying and scurrying with spices that must have been going on in the same way for thousands of years: coolies, dark-skinned and intense, trotting backwards and forwards with sacks on their backs; simple bamboo carts pulled by bright-eyed, shouting boys; warehouses piled to the ceiling with jute sacks bulging with aromatic contents—all watched over by the quiet but sharp middlemen sitting behind sample jars.

Who would have thought that this Malabar coast now exports some 15,000 tons of ginger per year? Much of this goes to Europe, the traditional market. An average European will consume a couple of ounces (50 g) of dried ginger per head per year, but only a tiny proportion of all that ginger ends up on the kitchen spice shelf. Most of it goes to the bakery industry for the production of ginger biscuits and cakes, but substantial amounts are processed into meat products, soups, pickles and chutneys. In addition, there is a growing market for ginger in soft drinks including, naturally, ginger beer. A little is still included in pharmaceuticals, especially throat and cough preparations.

So let us trace this ginger back to its source, and see what happens to it from there. As we have seen, ginger is grown in several areas of the world, the total production being at least 100,000 tons. In each area the ginger has its own characteristics of flavour, texture and traditional methods of preparing it for market. The table opposite shows the main variations according to source.

Forms of Ginger

As I have explained, when ginger is to be sold fresh, it is harvested early. Apart from trimming off the roots with little knives and cleaning, little is done to it before sale. Most of this *green ginger* is used in cooking in the countries where it is grown. Indeed, India itself uses at least 50,000 tons per year in this form. Some of it is kept for preserving in sugar and syrup. In the West very little

Table 1. Differing characteristics of ginger according to country of origin

SOURCE		APPEARANCE	TASTE
India	Cochin, unbleached	light brown, roughly peeled	lemony, rooty, fairly pungent
	Calicut, unbleached	red brown, roughly peeled	fairly lemony, rooty, fairly pungent
	Cochin/Calicut, bleached	white, lime coated	sweet, rooty, fairly pungent
Africa	Nigeria	dark, wrinkled, partly scraped	camphoraceous, harsh aromatic rooty and strongly pungent
	Sierra Leone	very dark grey-brown, wrinkled	earthy, camphoraceous, very pungent
Jamaica		light buff, smooth, clean peeled, hard	delicate, aromatic, spicy, mild pungency
China		pale brown, unpeeled	lemony, aromatic, mildly pungent
Australia		light brown, unwrinkled	strongly lemony, fairly pungent

ginger is sold in this way, most of it to the immigrant communities, where it can be found in local vegetable shops and, of course, in Chinese and Indian restaurants. Some of the green ginger is used in pickles and chutneys.

By far the most ginger is shipped from the growers already dried. This *dried ginger* is what most people are used to, for it ends up as the buff pungent powder in our spice bottles. After harvesting the fresh ginger, it is washed and the roots scraped off. Then it is laid out on clean floors and dried in the sun for a week to ten days, during which period it is turned occasionally, and piled up every night. If the fresh ginger is too fleshy and moist, the drying will take longer and it will end up looking shrivelled. This is one of the reasons why ginger for drying is harvested later, when it has lost more of its water.

Dried ginger is much stronger in taste and more pungent than fresh ginger. This extra strength is not only the result of a later harvest, which has allowed more time for the plant to accumulate flavours. It is also because the drying process itself seems to increase the pungent substances while reducing those that are lemony and aromatic. There is some evidence that, even when dry, the rhizome grows somewhat more pungent during short-term storage, although if ground and stored for extended periods, pungency decreases. Clearly this dry, wrinkled, dead-looking plant is alive and kicking somewhere inside!

In some places ginger is soaked overnight in the villages and rubbed clean. Then the corky outer skin is peeled off by hand with sharp knives before drying, to produce a clean and smooth dried ginger of superior quality. It has to be done carefully, as the tissues that contain the aromatic essential oil lie just under the skin, and a rough peeling will drastically reduce the aroma and taste. This is still done in Jamaica and in Kerala in India, but it is a disappearing skill, and unnecessary if the dried ginger is to be ground into powder.

Today the food and beverage industry often needs a more concentrated ginger flavour. It is not so easy to add ginger powder to a soft drink—you will end up with a muddy, turbid product. So ginger is extracted and concentrated. In this way it is also clean and free of bugs and dirt. One way is to extract dried ginger with a solvent such as alcohol or acetone (nail polish remover). Then the fibrous residue is thrown away and the solvent carefully evaporated off under a vacuum to leave a thick paste. This is called an *oleoresin*; it contains most of the flavour of the original ginger packed into one-fifteenth of the weight. It is strong stuff: only small amounts need be added to food products. Another way of concentrating the flavour is to get out the *essential oil*. This is done by bubbling steam through a mash of ginger, after which the oil is collected by distillation. It is highly concentrated—one gets around one part oil from 40 parts fresh ginger—but it is very aromatic, sweet rather than pungent, and full of flavour. It is popular, for example, in soft drinks.

One other traditional way of preparing ginger is to preserve it in sugar. It is that brown sugary, aromatic and spicy chocolate-covered sweetmeat, or the crystallised, brown, tasty sliver on top of the birthday cake. The sweet ginger pieces in sugar are known as *crystallised* or *stem ginger* (this is more accurate than it seems, for the ginger rhizome is indeed a stem, not a root). The brown syrup in which the pieces are bathed is known as *ginger syrup*. These ginger products have lost most of their medicinal ingredients and are therefore not effective medicinally. They are made in the Far East, where for centuries they have been the most popular form of sweet, and also in Australia.

The process starts with fresh ginger which is diced and then cooked in acid to soften the fibres and allow the sugar entry into the tissues. The repeated cooking turns the ginger brown, removes the aromatic oils completely, and reduces the pungency. It is then soaked in hot sugar solution for several days, continually replacing the sugar syrup and adding more sugar to make it gradually more concentrated. This eventually produces a syrup with diced, syruped ginger pieces in it, which is exported and used in all kinds of pickles, jams and marmalades, or packaged in decorative jars for the Christmas market.

How are candied crystallised ginger pieces made? Those with a sweet tooth and a strong imagination are invited to dream up all kinds of sticky processes. In fact it starts with the same ginger syrup. The sugar syrup is drained off, leaving the ginger pieces.

These are briefly washed and dried. They are then quickly dipped in a very thick sugar solution and immediately rolled in dry sugar several times. The results are mild-tasting, crystallised brown chunks that bear little resemblance to the original, knobby, pungent ginger 'hands'.

CHAPTER 6

The Chemistry of Ginger

It is always an exciting business to look inside a living plant, with its aromas and flavours, its strange effects on our bodies, and odd peculiarities yet to be discovered. This is the role of the natural product chemist. He attempts to understand some special quality of the plant through analysing its chemical constituents. His tools are those of the chemistry laboratory, which today includes some very sophisticated computer-controlled processes with exotic-sounding names: high pressure liquid chromatography, thin layer chromatography, gas chromatography, mass spectroscopy, nuclear magnetic resonance, and so on.

The analysis proceeds in this way. The plant is ground up, and an extract is made with water. Then a number of simple 'kitchen' tests are applied both to the solution containing the water-soluble constituents, and to the residue. These may include, for example, the use of dyes to estimate how much starch, fat and protein it contains. Or the whole plant material may be burned to an ash and then the minerals in the ash analysed in a simple apparatus, or the insoluble fibrous residue dried and weighed. Such tests give information on basic constituents but will tell us nothing about any special chemicals which might be there.

In the next stage, the chemist distils the essential oils in the plant, or extracts all the alcohol-soluble constituents. These liquids may contain hundreds of chemicals, so they are separated into groups by special 'fractionation' equipment, which selects chemicals according to their size or chemical nature. Then they are put through the analytical equipment to create a typical trace or pattern, which can be compared to that of known chemical compounds. In this way, single compounds are identified. Often unusual compounds are found, and the chemist hopes that these might be the cause of the unique property of the plant. If so, perhaps this will lead to the discovery of a new medicine, or flavour or odour.

Ginger Disintegrated

So, let us examine ginger, looking first at the major substances that the plant contains: the composition as opposed to the analysis. Fresh ginger, like any underground root or rhizome crop such as potato or carrot, consists mostly of water: about 80 per cent of its weight is water. There is around 2.3 per cent protein, and one per cent fat. The main solid component, again like a potato, is carbohydrate, or starch. This is present at around 12 per cent. It increases in the more mature ginger which has spent longer in the ground. Then there is about 2.5 per cent fibrous material, which also rises in the more mature ginger, and 1.2 per cent minerals—mainly calcium, phosphorus and iron. The vitamins too are nothing exceptional. A good supply of B vitamins, particularly thiamine, riboflavin and niacin, is combined with a healthy dose of vitamin C. However, since only small amounts of ginger are consumed, its nutritional content is unimportant relative to all the other constituents in the diet. As mentioned in chapter 1, ginger or other spices are not generally viewed as nutrients. Rather, it is in their unusual non-nutritive components that their value to us lies.

Dry ginger contains only about ten per cent moisture instead of the 80 per cent in fresh ginger. Therefore the amounts of all the other solid constituents are some three to four times greater in a given weight of fresh ginger.

Now let's go deeper and look at these special compounds. They are in two groups and are found in two places within the rhizome.

There is the essential oil of ginger. This is the aromatic oily liquid which is found in tiny vessels just under the corky skin. This oil is called essential oil because historically it was thought to represent the sap or essence of the plant, like the blood of an animal. This is the oil which is collected by distillation, just as the oils of flowers are collected by perfumers, or the oils in mint or thyme rise up from a hot herb tea. The second group is the oleoresin, mentioned in the last chapter, which is located in specialised cells dotted around the fleshy interior of the rhizome, in between the starch cells. This oleoresin is indeed resinous, and it can only be extracted and concentrated by using alcohol or special solvents like ether.

Before revealing how much of the oil or oleoresin there ought to be, it is important to realise that all plants, even of the same species, are very variable: they are not stamped out of a mould. Ginger will vary greatly depending on where it is grown, what varieties are used, how long it is in the soil, what agricultural methods are used, whether it is scraped or not, how it is dried and processed, and so on. The main constituents, such as starch, can vary by 50 per cent from type to type. However, the special constituents, the oil and the oleoresin, can vary by 100 per cent. For example, the scraped ginger from Cochin, which is coated with lime to improve its appearance, has only 1.49 per cent essential oil. Much has been lost in the scraping. The African ginger has double the quantity of oil as the skin is left on and it is anyway a strong-tasting variety.

Oil of Ginger

The essential oil is rich in multitudes of different components, each of which contributes to its characteristic flavour and aroma. These compounds are, obviously, oily, and 'boil' or vaporise at quite low temperatures. That is why the aromatic oils in, for example, mint, vaporise as soon as hot water is poured on the leaves, to give that typical menthol aroma in the air. No one is quite sure why the plants make these aromatic substances, many of which are very complicated chemicals requiring a lengthy production line in the plant cells. It could be as protection against some insects, or to attract others, particularly bees and wasps, to pollinate the flower. It may be to deter goats and cattle (which seem to use these plants as medicine but not as food). Or they could be substances in the process of being converted to other substances, a kind of snapshot of the factory production line and the factory store of spare parts.

Some of the main compounds in oil of ginger include zingiberene, curcumene, bisabolene, sesquiphellandrene, pinene, myrecene, borneol and farnesene. There are many others, perhaps 30 in all. A particular group of components called citrals, including geraniol, limonene and neral, are interesting because they give a citric, lemony aroma to the oil. However, they are not present in the oil from dried ginger, something which we can confirm for ourselves: the dry ginger powder in the spice rack does not have the lemony aroma. Since these components are, however, present in fresh ginger, it seems that drying the ginger in the hot sun produces all kinds of changes in its chemistry, the loss of the citrals being the most noticeable to us. The Australian dried ginger, and to some extent the Cochin, are exceptions in that they do preserve some lemony aroma because of the special harvesting and drying methods used there.

In fact the oil in ginger from different places has very different aromas and can vary in the same place from harvest to harvest. The Cochin oil is described as 'sweet, warm, rooty spicy with distinct lemony note', Nigerian is described as 'harsh, warm, rooty spicy, distinctly camphoraceous', while Chinese is 'mild, aromatic, rooty, lemony'. These differences are reflected in very large variations in the chemical mix of the various oils, and it is the flavour chemist's job to try to link differences in aromas and tastes with differences in the amounts of particular chemicals in the oil. In Indian oil, the main constituent is zingiberene which may make up to 70 per cent of the oil. Yet in Japanese ginger oil this compound amounts to only a few per cent and others dominate, with the result that Japanese ginger is much more delicate and has a mild, fruity/rooty aroma.

The oils also change with time. We know that foods can change their taste during storage, and our sensitive palates will recognise if food tastes old. When ginger oil or dried ginger is stored, various components change and react with others and the taste alters accordingly.

It is interesting that plants and flowers which contain essential oils do not have an infinite variety of chemical components to call upon. The number found in the plant world is limited, and the same chemicals crop up again and again in completely different types of plants. The aromas and flavours that we experience from basil, geranium, orange and ginger are the result of different selections and amounts of many of the same substances. For example, ginger oil contains pinene, geraniol, and limonene, discovered originally in the pine tree, geranium and citrus respectively.

Oleoresin

Distillation of aromatic plants to produce an essential oil is a traditional process, which has been known for millennia. During the last century chemically pure solvents such as alcohol became available. In 1879 a scientist by the name of Thresh extracted ginger with acetone, giving a brown liquid. When the acetone had dissolved away, he was left with a pungent, thick brown oily paste, the oleoresin. From this he managed to obtain the first pure chemical from ginger, a pungent substance which he named gingerol. Forty years later, in Japan, Dr Nomura made the next major contribution to ginger chemistry, finding in the oleoresin, firstly, the compound zingerone, and later another pungent compound which he called shogaol, after the Japanese word for ginger, *shoga*. The structure of these compounds, and others from the oil, is given in the diagram opposite.

More sophisticated work by a number of flavour chemists in recent years has delved deeper into these substances. Gingerol has been discovered to be, in fact, a number of gingerols; it is a group of very similar substances described as (6)-gingerol, (8)-gingerol and (10)-gingerol. The numbers refer to the length of a chain of carbon atoms on the side of the molecule. These three compose about a third of the oleoresin. The others, shogaol and zingerone, are also in groups of three, similarly described as (6)-, (8)- and (10)-shogaol and (6)-, (8)- and (10)-zingerone. Gingerol is the most pungent of the ginger constituents, followed by zingerone and then shogaol. It is interesting to note that, when stored, gingerol gradually changes to shogaol which, as you can see from the diagram, is not very different. This is why the pungency gradually drops as ginger powder sits, ageing, at the back of the kitchen cupboard.

There are other lesser components, such as (6)-, (8)- and (10)-paradol, (4)-, (6),- (8)- and (10)-gingediol; (6)-methylgingediol; (4)- and (6)-gingediacetate and hexahydrocurcumin. These contribute to, but do not determine the flavour and the medicinal effects of ginger.

Dietary Aids in Ginger

While we cannot expect ginger to contribute a great deal to our nutrition, it does help us to get the most out of our food. This is mostly because the medicinal components act as longshoremen or stevedores, carrying foods across the stomach wall and unloading them into the circulation. However, there are one or two

6 - Gingerol.

6 - Shogaol.

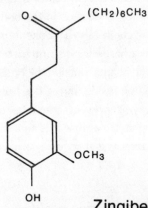

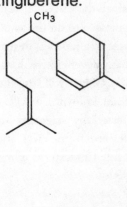

6 - Paradol.

Zingiberene.

Zingiberol.

interesting additional components in ginger that help in the diet. There is a considerable amount of protease. This is a catalytic substance similar to that used by the stomach to digest meat. As we mentioned in chapter 1, ginger is a good candidate for a commercial natural meat tenderiser. It would certainly help us to digest meat in our diet, and may be one of the reasons that the Chinese and other traditional cuisines include ginger with meat dishes. It also has a similar substance, a lipase, which helps to digest fats.

The other unusual components are anti-oxidants. These are compounds that prevent foods from going off or going rancid. Chemicals such as BHT or BHA are usually added to food products for this purpose. Ginger has been found to be the best of all the spices at preventing the oxidation of foods, and is even stronger than BHA. If it can prevent oxidation in foods, it may also be able to do the same in our bodies. Oxidation in the body creates free radicals, destructive rogue chemicals that contribute to many degenerative diseases, such as atherosclerosis, and hasten ageing. Ginger will stop these 'rogue elephants' outside the body. It is not known if it will to do the same inside, but it has been suggested by scientists that the way it prevents the rise of cholesterol in the circulation may be partly because it is an anti-oxidant. Cholesterol is more easily removed if it has not been oxidised.

Which Components are Effective as Medicines?

The most exciting part of all this chemical dissection is that it makes it possible to explore whether these individual substances can affect the body. By trying each one in turn on, say, the stomach, it is possible to decide which of this multitude of ginger substances actually calms the stomach. Eventually we may be able to catch a glimpse of how the various constituents act together to achieve the beneficial effects of the whole plant. This is never possible to do completely as the whole effect is built of the concerted harmonious action of a very large number of contributing chemicals. Even with the most intensively researched plants, such as garlic, this horizon is still far away. But a start can be made.

You might wonder why one should bother with all this chemical interference. Indeed, the identification of single chemicals in a plant does have a bad name among holistically and naturally minded folk. It is the way a safe plant remedy, rich in therapeutic substances, is 'boiled down' to a little white and toxic pill containing one single chemical. This is the main activity of the pharmaceutical industry. However, there is another practical purpose to the chemistry besides getting out the king chemical and selling him. If we discover which are the main active ingredients we can choose the best varieties, as well as monitor the strength and the consistency of plant remedies, without necessarily having recourse to little white pills.

In the case of ginger, time and again laboratory research has shown that the main medicinal components are not in the starches, minerals or water-soluble components, nor in the essential oil, but in the oleoresin. More than that, the research has pinned down the main active components to be the gingerols and shogaols, with minor contributions from the others.

Scientists at the Kyoto Pharmaceutical University have studied which components in ginger stopped vomiting and nausea. The vomiting reflex is controlled by the stomach's nervous system, which uses a messenger called serotonin to kick the stomach into the powerful contractions we call vomiting. It was discovered that the ginger oleoresin was much more effective than the oil in blocking this messenger. Dr Johji Yamahara and colleagues went further. They split the oleoresin into its components, tested them all and found that it was the gingerols that were mainly responsible for getting in the way of the serotonin messenger.

Ten years ago this research team had come to the same conclusion in relation to other actions of ginger. They found that it was the gingerols which were responsible for ginger's effects in stimulating the bile gland and the liver. Since this is one of the main cholesterol-clearing routes, it suggests that the gingerols could also be the cholesterol-reducing agents in ginger.

As we have already discussed, ginger inhibits the manufacture of prostaglandins, and this may be the way in which it warms the body and acts on the circulation. Researchers have shown that several compounds in ginger are mainly responsible for this. Some of them are the gingerols. But an additional series of substances in the oleoresin were found to be highly active in this way—indeed, much more so than the chemical indomethacin which is among the strongest of anti-inflammatory, prostaglandin-reducing drugs. These were the gingerdiones and the dehydroginger-diones. The interesting point is that these are the chemicals out of which gingerols are made by the plant cells. So it seems as if the whole chain of pungent ginger substances is acting together on the body.

Of course this is not the whole story. There are, presumably, situations in which other components of ginger come to the fore—for example, with colds and 'flu, when sweating is needed, traditional medicine suggests that fresh ginger is better. It is less pungent, but has more aromatic oils than the dried ginger. It is the oils, too, which are the reason why mint and basil tea are drunk for colds and 'flu. Obviously the pungent components do not do everything. However, now that we know that they are of central importance, we can confirm scientifically that dried ginger is better for stomach problems and anti-inflammatory and cholesterol-lowering effects.

Another conclusion is that the more pungent varieties of ginger are more medicinal. This means we should go for African ginger, or Indian ginger that is unpeeled. Peeling gives a nicer-looking rhizome, but reduces the potency. It is a peculiar fact that the British Pharmacopoeia always recommended Jamaica ginger for its medicinal syrups and ginger cough mixtures. This was because it looked better and was commonly regarded as being of a higher quality. Medicinal ginger was even called 'Jamaica Ginger' in some medical books. Yet we now know that Jamaican ginger, though better looking and more expensive, is in fact medicinally less effective than other varieties. Perhaps the Pharmacopoeia Commission should have consulted traditional herbalists rather than spice experts.

With our knowledge of the main active compounds in ginger, another door is opened. We can now check that those ingredients are actually present in any medicine, product or preparation of ginger. Suppose that I want to buy a bottle of ginger capsules or tablets. I might look on the label and read that the tablets contain ginger. However, it would be impossible to know how strong this ginger was. It could be very weak, or even have no medicinal components in it at all (for example if the tablet contained only the residues left over after someone had already extracted all the soluble components). I would simply have to trust the manufacturer. But how can the manufacturer himself know? Until it is clear which components are the medicinally active ones, even the manufacturer will have no idea what to look for when he buys the ginger to pack into the tablets.

All this is changed. A manufacturer now knows that he must make sure that there are plenty of gingerols and other pungent components in his tablets. If he does not have the analytical equipment to check this, he should ask his supplier of ginger powder or ginger extract to do the analysis and guarantee a certain ratio. It is possible today to purchase ginger extract which is standardised on the gingerols. That is, each batch of the ginger extract is guaranteed by analysis to have a similar amount of gingerols in it. So far only one extraction company, Botanicare, of Kiryat Shemona, Israel, is producing a ginger extract specially designed for medicinal uses and guaranteeing a constant amount of medicinally active components.

To get some idea of the richness of substances in ginger, you

Table 2.   Some biologically active compounds in ginger
         (*after J. A. Duke*)

SUBSTANCE	EFFECT
Asparagine	promotes urination
Borneol	analgesic, anti-inflammatory, lowers fever, liver protective
Chavicol	kills fungi
Cineole	anaesthetic, clears chest/throat infections and coughs, antiseptic, lowers blood pressure
Citral	antihistamine, antibiotic
Cumene	narcotic
Cymene	anti-flu, kills viruses, fungi, insects
Dehydrogingerdione	inhibits prostaglandins, treats liver
Geraniol	anti-candida, kills insects
Gingerdione	inhibits prostaglandins
Gingerols	analgesic, lowers fevers, stimulates circulation, lowers blood pressure, treats and calms stomach
Hexahydrocurcumin	treats liver, stimulates bile
Limonene	can irritate skin, deters insects
Linalool	prevents convulsions, antiseptic
Myrcene	kills bacteria, insects, relaxes muscles
Neral	kills bacteria
Pinenes	removes phlegm, kills insects
Shogaol	analgesic, lowers fevers, sedative, constricts blood vessels, raises blood pressure
Zingerone	raises blood pressure

may like to study a table prepared by Dr James A. Duke, one of
the world's leading experts on medicinal plants. He works in the
United States Department of Agriculture in Beltsville, Maryland.
The table, reproduced opposite, shows just how many substances
there are in ginger, all of which can have effects on our health.
The end result is a unique and complex action each time we take
ginger; a kind of symphony composed of the intermingling
sounds of all the separate instruments.

CHAPTER 7

History and Folklore

Once there was a baker who made a beautiful gingerbread boy. He rolled a dough containing plenty of dry ginger; he put in raisins for eyes and for the row of buttons on his little waistcoat. He put the boy into the roaring oven. When the boy was done he took him out on his peel. The gingerbread boy was a crusty nutty-brown colour, and smelt sweet, rich and aromatic. But as the baker was admiring him, the boy looked up and skipped off the peel. He glanced back, cheekily. 'I am the gingerbread boy and you can't catch me,' he teased, and off he ran, with the baker running after him, apron flapping in the breeze. As he ran through the village the cat saw him, and called out, 'Stop! Stop!' for he smelt delicious. But the boy just ran on, shouting, 'Run, run, as fast as you can, you can't catch me, I'm the gingerbread man!'

One by one all the domestic animals such as the cow and the cock, and eventually all the inhabitants of the village, tried to catch and eat the gingerbread boy, but they couldn't overtake him. At last he came to the river. As he was considering how to cross, the fox came up. 'I'll take you across,' he said. 'No, you'll eat me,' said the gingerbread boy. But the fox persisted, and by lies and whining pleas managed to persuade the gingerbread boy to ride on his back. Then, in midstream, the fox promptly finished him off.

If we look inside this well-known folk tale, we can witness the mercurial character of ginger. It is aromatic and delicious, attracting all who catch a whiff of it as it passes by. It also moves very fast. It warms up all who take it (that is, chase it) for they catch the same spirit of movement and are carried along by it. The tale is an allegory of ginger moving fast through the body, overcoming obstacles and warming up the system. Indeed, the image of the sleepy English village waking up and running in circles could not be a clearer metaphor for a stimulated circulation.

The gingerbread house is another feature of certain of our best loved folk tales. In *Hansel and Gretel* it is used by the evil witch to entice the children into her dwelling. Here the spicy aroma of ginger is equated with the eagerness and curiosity of the children, combined with the feeling that ginger is a homely spice that 'makes all things nice' and cannot therefore represent harm or danger.

Gingerbread has always been popular in England. Queen Elizabeth I liked it, and it has become traditional regional fare, acquiring different names in different localities. At the turn of this century it was called feridge in Norfolk, lollybanger in Somerset, parliament, scranchum or thickels in Northamptonshire. In the North of England and in Scotland, a gingerbread called parkin, using oatmeal instead of flour, was specially made for the celebration of November 5th. Gingerbread was important at country fairs and festivals. Gingerbread men were called husbands, with obvious reference to their warming qualities. Sometimes they were shaped like letters, or given (to quote W. T. Fernie, *Kitchen Physic*, 1901) 'whimsical devices, sometimes coarsely significant'. This even points to an erotic use for ginger.

Ginger, like all medicinal plants, has accumulated legends and folk tales that back up the belief in its medicinal powers. In traditional thought, all plants that help human beings are placed in the world by the deities as a boon. They do not, as the modern scientist would have it, appear by accident. For example, among the tribal people of its homelands, ginger is regarded as a vehicle of magical force and power. In East Papua it is used to heat up the body before casting spells. It is also chewed and spat out in order to ward off sudden squalls at sea, or spat onto the precious cargoes of the canoes in order to preserve them from harm. The anthropologist Bronislaw Malinowski, visiting the Tobriand Islands in 1915–18, found that the villagers used a species of wild ginger in rituals connected with the harvest and the storing of food. They would also spit ginger onto the places where roads entered their villages, in order to avert misfortune and hunger and encourage prosperity.

In medieval times, some people were so amazed at the wonderful aromas and tastes produced by ginger, as well as its other benefits, that they believed the plant was a direct export from Paradise. In 1305 Sire Jean de Joinville travelled to Alexandria in Egypt with Saint Louis. His writings tell us of the common belief of that time that the spices in Egypt came directly from the earthly Garden of Eden. Round it flow the four great rivers, the Ganges, Tigris, Euphrates and Nile, which carry the spices that fall into them. Where the Nile re-emerges on the surface of the earth, fishermen would stretch their nets in the evening, and in the morning would sometimes find them 'full of cinnamon, ginger, rhubarb, cloves, wood of aloes, and other such good things.'

Ginger's Venerable History

In 1972 was discovered in China the perfectly preserved tomb of the wife of the Prince of Tai, who died shortly after 168 BC. In it were bamboo cases and pottery jars containing a large number of foodstuffs, including ginger; other spices were cinnamon bark, pepper and galangal. This discovery provided some of the earliest evidence of the importance of ginger to the Orientals, and we can assume that in ancient times it formed as vital a part of their culture as it does today. Certainly all the old Chinese herbals mention ginger, the best known being the *Shen Nung Pen Tshao Tching*, or Manual of the Celestial Husbandman, a classic text recording a 5,000-year-old verbal tradition.

It was said of Confucius that he always liked to keep a side-dish of ginger by him when he ate. The earliest Chinese recipes, called the Eight Delicacies, were preserved from ancient times and written down, supposedly by Confucius, in the *Li Chi*, or Book of Rites. One of these reads, 'To make the grill, they beat the beef and removed the skinny parts. Then they laid it in a frame of reeds, sprinkled on it pieces of cinnamon and ginger, and added salt. It could be eaten thus when dried. Mutton was treated in the same way as beef, and also the flesh of elk, deer and muntjac.'

The literary evidence of the early centuries AD points to ginger being used as a seasoning for dried meat and fish, together with pepper, salt and salted beans. During the Tang Dynasty (AD 618–907) venison seasoned with ginger and vinegar was first recommended by the pharmacists (in the *Shen Meng* and *Ts'ang-Ch'i Ch'en*) as a tonic, but it came to be valued for its taste as well.

The Chinese enjoyed ginger sweetened with honey; when Marco Polo visited China in early medieval times he found honeyed and candied ginger being sold in the streets, especially at the onset of winter. They also flavoured tea with ginger and tangerine peel. Wine, which was generally made from rice or millet, was spiced with ginger, or sometimes with pepper, chrysanthemum, pomegranate flowers or saffron.

The Chinese were great traders across the China Seas and the Indian Ocean. The North African world traveller Ibn Battuta, writing in 1349, reported seeing their huge junks, each carrying a thousand men, with sails made of woven bamboo matting, in Calicut harbour on the south west coast of India. The sailors took their families with them on their two-year voyages and lived in comfortable quarters on board. 'The sailors live in their cabins with their children. They grow herbs for cooking, vegetables and ginger in wooden tubs . . . In all the universe there are no richer people than the Chinese.'

Customs have not changed: ginger is still used extensively in modern China in much the same way as in historical times. In the north it is a frequent ingredient in sauces for meat and fish, while in the south it is used more like a vegetable than a spice; some cooks include it in all meat dishes. It also plays its part in rituals. In Hong Kong, ginger is offered in the various temples. One traveller writes: 'Ginger hung in huge paper constructions offered to the deity acquires the power of increasing fertility. It is then auctioned off at the next Voluntary Association feast. The buyer will have a son within the year if he follows all the rules of conduct in relation to the deities and to the Society.'

In the West ginger has been known as long as there has been trade with the East. This goes back a long time. There were ships sailing from the Malabar coast of India to Arabian ports several thousand years ago, from where spice caravans brought the spices up to Egypt. Such a caravan, with its crew of Ishmaelites, picked up Joseph and brought him to Egypt some 3,500 years ago, and the spice trade across the Middle East is mentioned many other times in the Bible.

Ginger in the Classical Age

Spices always represented a measure of sophistication. Whoever could afford to flavour his food with exotic spices, brought at considerable expense from far away, was sure of his place in the superior classes. Thus they were sought after by all cultures. Empires were built on this quest, including the British Empire. Indeed, the search for new tastes and flavours has been one of the significant forces impelling human expansion and development. The ancient Romans were avid consumers of spices along with all kinds of strange foods and medicines. They imported from the

Middle East and from India, either through Arab middlemen or by fitting out their own trading expeditions. Not that every Roman supported this quest for the exotic. Gaius Pliny, writing around AD 77 in his *Natural History* (Chap 12, 14), was one who disapproved, at the same time as giving us some interesting information about ginger:

> The root of the pepper-tree is not, as some people have thought, the same as the substance called gingiberi, or by others zingiberi, although it has similar flavour. Gingiberi is grown on farms in Arabia and Trogodytica; it is a small plant with a white root. The plant is liable to decay very quickly, in spite of its extreme pungency. Its price is six denarii a pound. It is remarkable that the use of pepper has come so much into favour. In the case of some commodities their sweet taste is their attraction, and in others their appearance, but pepper has nothing to recommend it in either fruit or berry. To think that its own pleasing quality is pungency and that we go all the way to India to get this! Who was the first person who was willing to try this on his food, or in his greed for an appetite was not content merely to be hungry? Both pepper and ginger grow wild in their own countries and yet they are bought by weight like gold and silver.

It seems that in Pliny's time the Romans imported their ginger from Yemen on the south-west coast of the Asian peninsula. This was a fertile and well-watered land prior to the bursting of the great dam at Marib in the sixth century AD. Later, around AD 150, Ptolemy speaks of it as being imported from Ceylon: 'The products of Ceylon are rice, honey, ginger, the beryl, nakinthos, metals of all sorts including gold and silver, and elephants and tigers.' Ginger appears in six recipes in the most famous Roman cookbook, that of Apicius, in the fourth to fifth century AD. Ginger was one of the few herbal medicines that the Roman doctors used to carry with them as they accompanied the legions on their marches. The others they found or grew locally.

This spice trade did not cease with the fall of the Roman Empire, and churchmen continued to bring or dispatch medicinal substances, including ginger, to England and Europe. In seventh- and eighth-century France, Marseilles was a key port for the import of spices, being exempted from taxes by the Merovingian kings. In the ninth century, we find the monks of Corbie planning to buy numerous spices in the market in Cambrai in north-east France: these included pepper, ginger, cinnamon, galangal, myrrh, thyme, cloves, sage and mastick. Then came the rise of Islam, and the Moghul emperors found themselves governing the spice lands of the East. Arab traders held a monopoly over the spice trade for centuries.

The Arabian Nights

Ginger has always had a strong presence in the Arab world. It appears in the Koran: 76, 15–17. Muhammed in his younger days was a spice trader and among Arab merchants the dealers in spices were the aristocrats. They were trading in the exotic. Ginger appears often in Arabic poetry, and in the stories of *The Arabian Nights* it features as an aphrodisiac. Anything that heats the blood can be an aphrodisiac, especially in the luscious, erotic world depicted in those stories.

Many Arab merchants settled permanently on the south-west coast of India, the Malabar coast, with its great ports of Quilon, Cochin and Calicut where there was an extensive trade in ginger. Benjamin of Tudela, who travelled from Spain in 1160–73, gives the following description:

Thence it is seven days' journey to Khulan [Quilon] which is the beginning of the country of the Sun worshippers. These are the sons of Cush, who read the stars and are all black in colour. They are honest in commerce. When merchants come to them from distant lands and enter the harbour, three of the King's secretaries go down to them and record their names and then bring them before the King. Whereupon the King makes himself responsible even for their property, which they leave in the open unprotected. Pepper is found in that country. They plant the trees thereof in their fields and each man of the city knows his own plantation. The trees are small and the pepper is white as snow. And when they have collected it they place it in saucepans and pour boiling water over it, so that it may become strong. Then they take it out of the water and dry it in the sun, and it turns black. Cinnamon and ginger and many other kinds of spices are found in this land.

Ginger in Europe

Ginger has always had a close association with pepper. During the long centuries of the spice trade between Asia and Europe, pepper was commonly the most important commodity, with ginger running second.

The history of ginger in the Middle Ages is the history of the spice trade, with the different routes to and from the East rising and falling in importance, but always maintaining a healthy activity—the sea routes via Arabia to Europe, and the great overland caravan routes through Turkey and Persia, or through Turkestan and Russia. Spices were used to preserve and flavour foodstuffs, and as medicines. They had great status value in society, and prices for spices imported to Europe could reach high levels. Taxes were sometimes paid in pepper, and in ginger also: in medieval Aix the Archbishop taxed the Jewish community in pepper, ginger and wax for their right to have schools and cemeteries. In medieval Basel, the street where the Swiss traders sold spices was called Imbergasse, meaning Ginger Alley.

It was in order to find the secret sources of the spices, which until that time had been controlled by the Arabs, that the Portuguese and Spanish kings sent out Magellan, Vasco da Gama, Columbus and many lesser known explorers, who for the first time charted the globe. Around the beginning of the sixteenth century the Portuguese controlled the oceans, and therefore the rich pickings of the spice trade. They also conquered the Malabar coast of India, in particular Goa. Then, within fifty years, the Spanish imported ginger to the West Indies, where it grew with even greater flavour and abundance. Then the Dutch and after them the British took over and dominated the Indian and Malaysian trade. Spices came up to London via the Suez Canal, and London became a major spice centre. Dockland warehouses were stacked with the same aromatic cargo in gunny sacks that crowded the streets of Cochin.

Ginger appears again and again in English literature of all periods; it was a common household item, although it may have been reserved for special occasions. Chaucer, in the *Romance of the Rose*, describes a wonderful garden:

> There was eke wexyne many a spice
> As clowe-gelope, and lycorice,
> Gyngevre, and greyn de Paradys,
> Canell, and setewale of prys,
> And many a spice delitable
> To eten whan men rise fro table.

'Clowe' is of course, cloves; 'canell' is cinnamon, and 'setewale', later known as 'setwall', is the old word for zedoary. Shakespeare mentions ginger several times. In *The Winter's Tale* a feast is prepared and plans are laid to borrow 'a race of ginger' from the neighbours. In *Love's Labour's Lost* Costard announces: 'And I had but one penny in the world, thou shouldst have it to buy gingerbread.' In *The Merchant of Venice* Salanio quips: 'I would she were as lying a gossip in that as ever knapped ginger.' Ginger is 'knapped' or snapped into pieces. Is this the origin of the well-known ginger snaps?

A wonderful English use of ginger was for spicing up beer or porter. For centuries a jar of ginger would be placed on the counter of taverns, for customers to help themselves. It was especially spicy when the beer was also warmed with a hot poker.

Ginger in the Western Herbal Tradition

The herbalists in the West certainly respected and used ginger, though not to the extent that it was used in China and India, where the plant is indigenous. It all started, as one might have expected, with the Greeks, who acquired their ginger from Arab spice merchants and soon discovered its medicinal power. Pythagoras is said to have recommended it as a digestive and carminative. Galen, the true father of modern medicine, was impressed with ginger's heating properties: 'It creates heat powerfully, but not immediately at first contact like pepper.' In other words, it generates a more gentle but longer lasting fire.

In ancient Rome ginger was one of the ingredients of the *Mithradaetum*. This was a compounded remedy created by the physicians to King Mithradates of 80 BC, as a protection against poisoning. It became one of four main remedies of the Roman period, the Four Official Capitals.

European herbalists all looked back to the classical period for

91

instruction and inspiration to which they added their own discoveries. The most famous Renaissance herbalist, Gerard, writes typically that: 'Ginger, as Dioscorides reporteth, is right good with meat in sauces, or otherwise in conditures; for it is of an heating and digesting qualitie, and is profitable for the stomacke, and effectually opposeth it selfe against all darkness of the sight . . . ' Gerard actually tried to grow ginger in England, but he sadly reported that it was killed by frost. Presumably he did not have the benefit of a sunny south-facing conservatory.

This was also the high period of Arabic medicine, and naturally, as the Arabs were the spice merchants of Europe, ginger figured largely in their medicine chests. In a guide called *The Medicine of the Prophet*, by Al Sayuti of Cairo, who lived in the latter part of the fifteenth century, we read: 'Ginger is hot and dry in the third degree, and dry in the second. It contains [that is, prevents] excess of damp. It is an aid to digestion, strengthens sexual intercourse and dissolves wind. If the purge Turbith [a common medieval laxative] is weak, or if there is oedema, then its reaction is strengthened by the addition of ginger. It renders fluid the thickness of phlegm. A confection of ginger soothes the stomach. It is a help in old age.'

We have already mentioned how King Henry VIII, in one of many regal manias, insisted that the Lord Mayor of London use ginger against the plague. He was not the only royal personage with a ginger obsession. Queen Elizabeth I had a famous 'pother' or powder, which was composed chiefly of white ginger, together with lesser amounts of cinnamon, caraway, anise, and fennel powders, which she took 'at anietime after or before meate, to expel winde, comfort ye stomach, and help digestion.'

We can recognise in these traditional uses the same themes as those we have discussed in the previous chapters, and which are mostly confirmed by modern research: that ginger warms the body, improves and stimulates the circulation, and is one of the main stomach remedies. Some beneficial consequences of this are also mentioned: better circulation and body function in old age, and improved sex life. This is obviously linked to body heat and the circulation. We even describe a sexually active person as 'hot blooded'.

The History of the Word 'Ginger'

The word 'ginger' has passed largely unaltered through the Indo-European languages—that is, all the languages of the European group including Greek and Latin. In Greek it is *ziggiberis*; in Latin *zingiber*; in French *gingembre*; in Spanish *jenjibre*; in German *Ingwer*; and in English ginger. These all derive from the Sanskrit, which is the mother of the Indo-European languages. The Sanskrit word for ginger is *sringa-vera*, meaning 'antler-shaped', which in turn comes from a Dravidian root, a prehistoric form of Malayan, in which ginger is *inchi-ver*. In Arabic it is *zanjabil*, and Hebrew *zangvill*. These languages have a Mesopotamian or Egyptian root; however in this case they have borrowed the term, along with the spice itself, from the East.

In modern Hindi, ginger is known as *Ada*, or *Adrak*, or *Adrakam* in related dialects. However, this applies to fresh ginger only. Dried ginger is known as *Sunthi*.

CHAPTER 8

Preparations, Potions and Products

There is little doubt that in general the best way to take any herb is fresh and unprocessed. When I need to use a particular herb, I go out into the garden and pick the leaves or root, and use it straight away. It is then that I thank my lucky stars for the investment in labour that has gone into my herb garden. The main reason is that I know what I am getting. If I bought the same herb from a shop, either as dried leaves or a tablet, I would probably trust that it was the correct species (although I would have no way of knowing even this), but I could not be so sure that it was fresh enough or whether it had lost some of its active components through age. I would not know if it was grown in the best way and was of the most medicinally active variety. It is also possible that it might contain contaminations or be of a lower dosage than it appeared.

You may rightly say that a reputable supplier of herbal remedies would not monkey around with contaminated or degraded herbal stock. This is very true. But the problem is that many suppliers of herbal products do not themselves have the technical ability to analyse and check that the herbs are really the best. For example, a shipment of ginger powder arriving from the East may look exactly as it should. Yet someone in the Far East may have already partly extracted or removed some of the active ingredients, leaving largely residue. This does happen, and only a laboratory could detect it. Almost all the feverfew herb tablets sold in North America have little in the way of active ingredients, less than a tenth of those contained in the feverfew sold in the United Kingdom. This is because the wrong variety was used in the first place for the agricultural stock. Yet the plant looked exactly the same. Again, only a laboratory could tell.

With ginger one is a little better off, because one can actually taste the active ingredients. They are the pungent components, so that if the ginger tastes pungent it is probably good. With other herbs one is not so fortunate. You would have to be a real herbal sage to taste the difference between good quality and bad in the case of ginseng, eleuthero, echinacea, and indeed most herbs.

It is also easy to make sure you are getting the correct plant if you can see the whole rhizome. However, this is not the case if you use powder. Ground ginger does get adulterated with substances like flour and chalk. In one investigation by the Inland Revenue in Ottawa, Canada, 150 samples of ground ginger were tested in the laboratory. Of these 21 were adulterated and 14 more were doubtful. Even adulterated ginger or ginger that has had its soluble ingredients stolen *en route* may taste pungent, for someone has invented the mean trick of adding hot pepper powder to ginger residue to make it seem pungent. Another problem that is specific to ginger and medicinal foods is that they are occasionally full of bacteria, fungi and even insects; or if not, they may have the chemical residues of treatments that killed the fungi and insects, which is probably worse.

Where does this leave us? I suggest two options:

- As mentioned above, you can try to obtain fresh ginger from your vegetable suppliers, or dried ginger in whole 'hands' from an ethnic food store. You can grind the latter at home in a coffee grinder or mortar and pestle.

- Alternatively, you can purchase medicinal ginger tablets at your health store. In that case, as with all herbs, you should look for products marketed by the most reputable and expert company. The product may contain ginger powder or ginger extract. Both are equally effective, the extract being more concentrated and cleaner. Unquestionably, the best product would be one which is standardised, that is guaranteed by analysis to contain a proper level of active ingredients. As the main active ingredients are gingerols, you should look on the packet for a promise that the product contains a given level of gingerols. Seven Seas Health Care Ltd makes such a product for the British market.

Less advisable is to purchase the ground spice from a food store, even if it may be somewhat cheaper, for the reasons described above. However, if you have no choice, try to purchase the ground ginger from an ethnic food store rather than from your local supermarket, on the supposition that the local immigrant community would be more discriminating as to quality.

Dosage

In Chinese medicine, ginger is given at a minimum dose of three grams of dried ginger per day, going up to ten grams. This is a little higher than would be recommended for self-treatment, and is used by professionals, such as herbalists or those with professional experience, for the treatment of health problems.

Readers of this book will be mostly non-professional, however, and will want to use ginger as part of their family medicine chest. It will be used as part of general self-care, for minor symptoms, such as stomach upsets or nausea, that may crop up day by day. In such cases the usual dose is one gram of dried ginger per dose, or about one-fifth of a teaspoon of dried ginger. This corresponds to about 100 mg of concentrated ginger extract in pill form. In the case of fresh ginger, the equivalent dose would be about four grams, or a flat teaspoonful. You can take up to four doses per day as necessary.

In the case of a ginger extract, it is difficult to give precise dosage guidelines without having the product in front of us, for extracts can be prepared in a number of different ways. You would do best to be advised by the manufacturer's recommendations. It should be an amount equivalent to a maximum of one gram of dried ginger per dose. It may also be a little less, so that there is more opportunity to vary dosages by taking a number of tablets. There should be a note on the packet describing the equivalent of the recommended dose in terms of ground ginger.

In the British Pharmacopoeia of 1973, an alcoholic extract is described, called a 'Strong Ginger Tincture'. This is prepared by steeping 500 g of ginger powder in one litre of 90 per cent alcohol. The dose is given as 0.5 ml. This would be equivalent to only one-quarter gram of ginger, a very low dose for therapeutic purposes. However, this was because it was mostly used by pharmacists for flavouring rather than as a medicine. In Martindale's *Extra Pharmacopoeia* the dosage is given as one-quarter to one gram per dose.

Making Ginger Potions and Preparations

Ginger Oil
This is a very useful remedy for headaches and painful joints or muscles. It is made simply by mixing one part of the juice of grated ginger to five parts sesame oil. The mixture is then rubbed in. You can use it to treat earache by putting one or two drops on some cotton wool and then letting it spread into the ear.

Ginger Compress and Ginger Bath
Put 100 grams of finely grated fresh ginger in some cheesecloth. Put that in a bowl containing one litre of hot water (below boiling, at around 70 degrees C). Keep at this temperature for a while until the water turns yellow (you can heat it a little). Soak a

97

towel in this liquid and apply repeatedly to the skin, as hot as you can bear. Warm the liquid again when it cools down.

When the skin goes red the compress has done its job and the circulation has been stimulated in that area. It is useful for pains, swellings, inflammations, joint problems, and even some internal conditions, especially bronchial problems when applied to the chest.

Ginger Poultice and Plaster
Poultices are warm, moist pastes of herbs and other powders which are placed on the skin to relieve inflammation, boils and eruptions, bites and stings. Poultices of plantain, comfrey or marshmallow can draw out toxins and heal infections; catnip, lobelia and echinacea can relieve pain and cramps. Ginger can be added to all of these poultices to promote the circulation in the affected area, and help the other herbs to get inside and do their job.

A ginger plaster, consisting of a paste of grated ginger and bread or tofu inside muslin, can be placed on the skin to relieve local inflammations and draw out fever. A very effective poultice to relieve pain and inflammation and promote circulation in rheumatic and arthritic conditions consists of:

Dry ginger root—2 parts
Cayenne pepper—1 part
Lobelia—½ part

Tea for Cramps and Spasms
Cramp bark, as its name suggests, is a useful herb against cramps and spasms. Michael Tierra, who suggested the previous formula, has proposed that a tea made of one part ginger and two parts cramp bark would be the optimal mixture, or alternatively, a tea of equal parts ginger and chamomile. It goes well with the ginger compress described above for external application.

Laxative Mixture

Laxatives such as senna, cascara or rhubarb root are quite strong; they may cause stomach cramps or pains and reduce the effectiveness of digestion. Therefore if you take such laxatives, add ginger at about 50 per cent of the laxative dose to protect the digestion. This is not necessary with bulk-forming laxatives such as flax seed (linseed) or psyllium. Other aromatic carminatives, such as fennel and aniseed, may be helpful.

Chinese Warming Formulae

Chinese formulae are individually designed to take into account the specific imbalances that lead to disease in a particular individual. Therefore it is hard to give general formulae that will be appropriate for everyone. Instead, you should obtain a prescription from a professional practitioner who will design a mixture especially for each individual.

Ginger Tea for Fevers and Colds

This is a classic standby to encourage sweating and bring out low grade fevers and colds (see chapter 4):

Grate a small piece of fresh ginger of about one gram (about the size of half a sugar cube) into a glass. Add lemon juice from about half a lemon, fill with hot water and add a little honey to sweeten.

Ginger Miso Revival Soup

For recovery and recuperation, and also as a nutritious and warming soup during illness:

Dissolve a level teaspoonful of miso in a cup of hot water, or better, vegetable stock. Add a dash of good shoyu sauce, chop in some spring onions, and grate in a piece of fresh ginger of roughly two grams.

Trikatu

This is the classic Ayurvedic recipe for the digestive system. It is used for nausea, indigestion, poor appetite, colic, wind, candida, coughs and colds, poor circulation and for removing toxins. It is better for Kapha and Vata constitutions and types of problems than for Pitta types.

Ginger, black pepper and long pepper (*Piper longum*) are combined in equal parts, either as powders or, when mixed with honey in the Ayurvedic fashion, made into pills. One to three grams are taken two or three times a day. This formula can be adapted by replacing the long pepper with aniseed, to make it gentler, especially for children. Alternatively coriander, nutmeg and ajwan (celery seed) can be added to enrich the formula and make it milder.

Yogi Tea

This is the classic Indian warming tea, nutritive, digestive, calming and clearing to mind and body. It is taken by mountain people to keep warm and revive their spirits.

2 teaspoonfuls fresh grated ginger

4 whole cardamoms

8 whole cloves

1 stick of cinnamon

8 cups of water

Boil until the liquid is reduced by half. Add half a cup of milk.

Ayurvedic Tea for Colds

This is a classic Indian remedy for the treatment of colds, catarrh, congestion, the beginning of influenza or other viral disease. It helps the immunity and warms the body:

3 cm piece of ginger, grated

3 cm piece of liquorice, chopped

5 peppercorns

A few leaves of tulsi, Indian holy basil (you can substitute sweet basil if tulsi is unavailable).

2 cups of water

Boil until the liquid is reduced by half.

The Pharmacists' Laxative

Pharmacists have a laxative mixture containing rhubarb, peppermint, ginger and gentian, which is a sensible mixture, combining the laxative element (rhubarb) with ginger, to improve digestion and remove nausea, peppermint, to prevent cramps and pain, and gentian to stimulate the appetite and the liver. This recipe is from the National Pharmaceutical Union, London, 1966, published in Martindale's *Extra Pharmacopoeia*:

Strong ginger tincture (50 grams dried ginger steeped in 100 ml alcohol)—0.15 ml

Sodium bicarbonate—½ gram

Peppermint oil—0.03 ml

Concentrated rhubarb infusion—0.6 ml

Concentrated compound gentian infusion—0.5 ml

Water (they say chloroform water) to 15 ml

The above is one dose.

How Safe is Ginger?

We can assume that ginger is very safe indeed. After all, it is a food substance used all over the world in the diet for breakfast, lunch and supper. Ginger is on the spice shelves of your local supermarket, without a Government health warning on the label, and there are other things there for which such a label is far more necessary. Nevertheless, it is worth checking scientifically.

Research has indeed confirmed ginger's safety. Animals have been given daily amounts of ginger equivalent to a human being consuming 3.5 Kg (about 7.5 lbs) per day without noticeable ill-effects. When pure gingerol or shogaol is given to animals they can cope with 250 mg per Kilogram, equivalent to about 2 Kg (4.4 lbs) of ginger for a human.

An extensive survey of the world medical literature has failed to come up with reports of side-effects from taking ginger as a food or a medicine, and none are given in the national drug guides, the pharmcopoeias, in which ginger is mentioned. Indeed, the US Food and Drug Administration has classed ginger along with the safest of herbs, in the Generally Recognised As Safe (GRAS) category. This allows it to be on open and general sale.

So we know that ginger is completely safe. However, we should also be aware that any food, when taken by the wrong person in the wrong way, can have adverse effects. Carrots are safe, but someone taking too much carrot juice, especially if he or she has a liver problem, may get a vitamin A overdose. In the case of ginger, it would be a mistake to take it during a high fever. Similarly, if there are other symptoms of hot conditions, ginger is not recommended. Such symptoms include dryness with a rapid pulse, red skin, a bright red tongue, dehydration, or blood in the stools. It does not turn ginger into a raging poison, but it could accentuate the symptoms of overheating.

CHAPTER 9

Spice up Your Cooking with Ginger

Ginger is the symbol of the merging of the kitchen cupboard and the medicine cabinet. In a holistic sense the entire field of medicine needs to be brought back in to life. By that I mean that it needs to re-enter our world as a normal, natural influence, such that there is no essential difference between a draught of clean water that satisfies our thirst and a herbal brew that treats a potential health problem.

From that perspective there is no conflict in cooking with our medicines, and none in including recipes for lunch in a book on herbal remedies. So this chapter will look at some of the ways in which ginger can be included in our normal diet. Of course this is not a cookery book, so the recipes will be 'tasters' rather than the full menu.

As I mentioned in chapter 1, the amounts of ginger or other spices included in such recipes will not be sufficient to cure diseases. But they will have a range of gentle and long-term health benefits such as warming the body, clearing toxins, promoting digestion and elimination, improving the absorption of nutrients, preventing food poisoning and rancidity, helping to prevent atherosclerosis, and so on. In other words, cooking with medicinal foods like garlic, ginger, aniseed, linseed, fenugreek, mustard, cinnamon, caraway or thyme and mint will generally have a preventative rather than curative health role.

Meat Dishes

Ginger is a classic addition to meat dishes throughout Asia, particularly because it helps to predigest and absorb the meat. It should be even more important these days, because the health status of factory-farmed, pesticide-loaded meat seems dire. I myself have been a vegetarian for many years, so I cannot claim familiarity with cooking meat. However, I am so familiar with the use of spices, especially after two years in India, that I feel safe in recommending one or two ideas.

All steaks will benefit from being rubbed all over with fresh ginger before and during braising and grilling. So will chicken. For example, before roasting chicken, rub all over with a paste consisting of a 5 cm piece of fresh ginger, 2 cloves of garlic and salt ground together.

The following is a typical Chinese ginger steak:
    1 Kg rump or sirloin steak
    30 g sesame or other oil
    2 onions and 2 garlic cloves
    5 cm piece of fresh ginger
    salt and pepper
    soy sauce
Fry the onions and crushed garlic and, when golden brown, add the ginger finely chopped, and cook briefly. Then add the meat cut into thin slivers, some soy sauce, the seasoning, and water. Bring to the boil and then cover and simmer until the meat is cooked.

Chicken Chow Mein is a classic Chinese dish that needs its ginger:
200 g noodles	2 cloves garlic
200 g chicken	1 inch piece of fresh ginger
200 g cabbage	2 teaspoons shoyu sauce

2 eggs	1 teaspoon chilli sauce
chicken stock	2 teaspoons tomato sauce
60 g mushrooms	2 teaspoons vinegar
2 leeks	1 cup oil

Cook the noodles until soft, wash and drain. Cook the chicken in the stock, and shred it. Fry the crushed garlic, leeks, cabbage, mushrooms, chopped ginger and shredded chicken. Add the chicken stock and the sauces. Fry the cooked noodles briefly, add the chicken-vegetable mixture, and garnish with beaten eggs, also fried.

Fish Dishes

A simple Chinese-style ginger fish dish can be prepared by marinating fish in a sauce of 2 tablespoons of sherry, segments of spring onions, ½ teaspoonful of dried ginger and salt. The fish can then be fried, after which it is sprinkled with coarse ground pepper and garnished with lemon.

Another strong ginger sauce consists of 1 tablespoonful of shoyu sauce, 1 teaspoonful of sesame oil, 1 teaspoonful of dried ginger or, preferably 1 tablespoonful of chopped fresh ginger. This is poured over the cooked fish before serving. Garnish with spring onions.

Vegetable Dishes

Indian dishes will often contain ginger along with other spices in the *masala*, meaning spice mixture. In some regions, and particular in the colder areas, ginger becomes the dominant note. Very often meat and vegetables are transposable in Indian cooking, with the same basic procedure in use.

Try adding dry ginger to rice when it has just finished cooking. Both cinnamon and ginger add an aromatic zest to plain rice. Rice can also be enriched by cooking it with cinnamon sticks, nuts and raisins, and a bay leaf or two, which you put in with the cold water at the beginning. Then sprinkle it with ginger before serving.

One of my regular favourites is *channa masala*, spiced chickpeas:

250 g chickpeas	1 teaspoon coriander
1 tablespoon dry mango powder	2 teaspoons garam masala
	2 inch piece of ginger
1 teaspoon cumin powder	vegetable oil
1 teaspoon red chilli powder	red or green peppers
	salt

Soak the chickpeas overnight and then cook until soft. Strain and keep the liquor. Mix the spices and some salt with the cooked chickpeas, and sprinkle with the garam masala. Grate the ginger, chop the peppers, and add them to the chickpeas. Now fry the oil, or ghee if you can get it, and when hot, add the chickpea mixture. Simmer for ten minutes, gradually adding a few teaspoonfuls of the left-over liquor.

Ginger goes very well with single vegetables cooked in butter or ghee. For example, you can melt butter, and then chop in cauliflower, thin slices from a 5 cm piece of fresh ginger, and salt. Cover and cook slowly, without water. Sprinkle with roughly ground black pepper when ready.

Potatoes and peas (*matar aloo*) make the classic simple household curry of northern India:

100 g shelled peas	1 inch piece of ginger
200 g potatoes	50 grams onion
125 g yoghurt	½ teaspoon coriander
oil or ghee	½ teaspoon chilli powder
salt	⅓ teaspoon turmeric
½ teaspoon ground cumin	powder

Heat the oil or ghee, slice and fry the ginger and onions, add the yoghurt (tomato puree is an alternative) and continue frying until the oil separates. Then add peas, potatoes, powdered spices and salt. Stir and fry gently for two minutes, then add water and cover, simmering until the potatoes are soft. Garnish with coriander leaves. A famous Indian dish called *matar panir* (peas and cheese) is made similarly, using just peas instead of peas and potatoes, and adding 200 grams of Indian cheese (or tofu).

Some vegetables can be cooked, sweetened or glazed with ginger. For example ginger sweet potatoes:

    4 sweet potatoes
    2 tablespoons butter
    2 tablespoons honey
    ¾ teaspoon ground ginger
    salt and pepper
    ½ cup of orange juice

Slice and cook the sweet potatoes, then layer in a buttered casserole, sprinkling each layer with salt, pepper and a little butter. Mix the rest of the ingredients and pour over the potatoes, and bake in a hot oven for about 20–30 minutes. A variation on this theme is possible with carrots. If the above is too sweet, try a mix of lemon juice, salt, pepper, ginger and butter on carrots before baking them.

Ginger Desserts

Ginger, like cinnamon, goes well with baked fruit and all kinds of desserts. It adds both aroma and a little extra pungency. Stem ginger, that is sweet preserved ginger, has always been used in desserts; however, it has little of the original pungent and aromatic constituents left.

Grapefruit tastes sublime when sprinkled with a mixture of

brown sugar or honey and ginger. The same goes for melon, which also requires some lemon juice for tartness.

Ginger ice-cream is one of the fringe flavours that attract their devotees. Here is a strong version:

    1 teaspoon ground ginger
    150 ml ginger syrup
    75 g preserved ginger
    275 ml cream
    150 ml prepared custard
    50 g castor sugar

Chop the preserved ginger and mix the gingers together. Half-whip the cream, and add all the rest of the ingredients. Chill, then freeze. A lighter version uses two whipped egg whites instead of the custard.

Ginger marmalade can be made by squeezing the juice of five oranges and slicing the peel. These are simmered together for at least an hour. Peel and core five cooking apples, and simmer. Add the cooked apples to the oranges, then add 3 Kg sugar, stirring until dissolved. Chop in 200 g preserved ginger and three teaspoonfuls ground ginger. Boil and, when ready to set, pour into jars. You can check if it is ready to set by dripping a little onto a plate. If it gels and forms a skin when cold, it is ready.

It is even easier to make apple and ginger jam as the apples contain more pectin and set without too much trouble. Make a syrup by boiling 2 Kg sugar in 2 litres water. Add 2 Kg peeled, cored, cut apples and 50 g grated ginger root. Simmer until clear and ready, and bottle. Various other fruits are suitable. You can try pears, gooseberries, rhubarb and peaches, which all go well with ginger.

Ginger Pumpkin Pies

One day in 1975, I was standing at a crossroads in Nepal with pack on back, maps in pocket, boots on feet, ready to trek across the mountains. The only question was, left or right. Left led to Pokhara, right to the Chinese border. The choice was radical. While musing, a baby-faced and lively American Peace Corps worker trotted by, and we chatted for a minute. I broached the options. He immediately responded that there was no contest; the Chinese border route was by far superior. 'There is a place called Dhulikel which you must visit,' he said decisively. I expected him to hold forth on the friendliness of the Sherpas, the beauty of the mountains, or the nature of the path, but he continued, 'At a certain crossroads there is a teahouse where you can get the best pumpkin pie this side of the Atlantic Ocean.' I did indeed get to savour this unique pumpkin pie, and I am now convinced that fresh green mountain ginger contributed to its magnificence. I approximate the recipe below:

Sift together 2½ cups of flour, 1 teaspoonful baking powder, 1 teaspoonful soda, 1 teaspoonful salt, ¾ teaspoonful cinnamon, 50 g grated ginger, ¼ teaspoonful cloves and 1 cup sugar. Add 1 cup brown sugar, 100 g butter or soft vegetable shortening, ½ cup buttermilk, 1½ cups cooked pumpkin. Beat for a short while, and add three eggs and beat again, and pour into two greased and floured flan tins. Bake in a moderate oven (180°C, 350°F, Reg. 4) until firm. Should take about 45 minutes.

Today, nearly 17 years on, I wouldn't eat such a heavy pumpkin pie. So I give the kind of recipe I would use now:

Make a basic pie crust of wholemeal flour, salt and water, sufficient to line an average round cake tin, adding some raisins and chopped nuts. Put this into the oiled baking tin and bake lightly. Boil 2 cups of pumpkin and puree it, add sufficient honey to sweeten, 2 tablespoons of tahini (sesame paste), ½ teaspoonful of cinnamon, ½ teaspoonful of ginger, or grate in a 3 cm piece of fresh ginger, and ¼ teaspoonful of cloves. Pour mixture into pie shell. Decorate with nuts and raisins and bake in a moderate oven for 30 minutes.

Pumpkin bread is also popular with my family and friends. For this, make a batter of wholemeal flour, salt and water. Add to this 1½ cups boiled pumpkin puree, one beaten egg, and stir. Add grated fresh ginger, cinnamon, a pinch of nutmeg and cloves. Add raisins and chopped nuts. Stir and thicken if necessary with more flour to make a thick batter. Pour into an oiled cake tin and bake in a hot oven (200°C, 400°F, Reg. 6) for about 45 minutes.

Gingerbread Men

This is the long-awaited recipe for healthy, holistic gingerbread men:

Mix together ½ cup oil or melted butter, ½ cup honey and ½ cup water. Stir in sufficient quantity of wholemeal flour to make a thick batter. Add 1 teaspoonful of salt and a dessertspoonful of ground ginger, as well as ½ teaspoonful each of cloves, cinnamon and allspice. Add enough flour to make a stiff dough and chill. Roll out thickly and, using a cardboard stencil or biscuit cutter if needed, cut out little men shapes. Use currants, raisins and nuts for the eyes, nose, buttons, and so on. Bake for 15 minutes in a moderate oven.

More traditional gingerbread can be made as follows:

100 g butter	¼ teaspoon each salt,
75 g brown sugar	cinnamon, allspice and
1 tablespoon marmalade	cloves

150 ml milk

200 g wholemeal flour

1 teaspoon bicarbonate of
soda

225 g golden syrup or honey

½ teaspoon ginger

2 eggs, well beaten

Warm the butter, sugar, marmalade, honey or golden syrup and the milk, and blend till smooth. Mix with the beaten eggs. Sift the flour, salt, spices and soda together, and gradually add the liquid ingredients. Mix to form a smooth batter and then pour into a baking tin and bake in a moderate oven for about one hour, or until ready.

Ginger biscuits are made somewhat similarly. Mix 400 g sugar and 300 ml honey or golden syrup. Melt 300 g butter and add, stirring in well, 1 tablespoonful ground ginger and 1 teaspoonful each cinnamon and cloves. Stir in 300 ml buttermilk, and mix in 1 Kg wholemeal flour, or use cream and plain flour for the traditional recipe. Make a thick dough, knead well, cover and leave in a cool place overnight, and then roll out and cut into biscuit shapes. Bake for about 15 minutes in a medium oven. Ginger snaps are a variation on this recipe, with a lot more soda, and also one egg, which makes them lighter and crisper.

Ales and Wines

Ginger beer, or ginger ale, is available in cans as a debilitated, saccharin, soft drink. If you want to taste the real thing, with the real taste of ginger, try this:

500 g sugar

2 large lemons

30 g fresh ginger, smashed well

1 teaspoon dried beer yeast

5–10 g cream of tartar

4 litres boiling water

Pour the boiling water on the sugar, ginger and cream of tartar. When cool add the rind and the juice of the lemons and the yeast. Ferment in a warm place, skimming off any yeast that rises to the surface. Strain or siphon into bottles which should not be tightly stoppered. Serve after at least a week.

Ginger wine is wonderful on a cold night, and it is a great digestive. You need:

    60 g fresh ginger, chopped and smashed
    500 g raisins, or equivalent in grapes
    1.5 Kg sugar
    2 large lemons and 2 large oranges
    ¼ teaspoon cayenne pepper
    1 sachet dried wine yeast and yeast nutrient if available

Boil the crushed ginger, the rind of the fruit and the pepper in the water. Stir in the sugar until dissolved, and then add the raisins, previously chopped. Start off the yeast by adding it to warm sugared water in a small jar, and leaving it for an hour or two. When the mixture is cool, add the juice of the fruit, fermenting yeast, and nutrients. After one week strain, and press the raisins. Continue fermentation, in a stoppered vessel with an air lock to let out the gases, until it is finished. This should be in about two weeks: the wine should be still, without any gassing. Allow the wine to stand until clear. Siphon off into bottles.

Punch is a spiced alcoholic or partially alcoholic drink, which absolutely requires ginger along with the clear, astringent aroma of cloves. It is based on red wine, one bottle going with about 100 grams of brown sugar, a dollop of rum, some orange and apple juice, a large piece of crushed ginger, half a dozen cloves, and a lemon or two. The mixture, with lemon rind, is warmed gently but never to boiling point. The juice of the lemon is added before serving.

Ginger Chutneys and Pickles

One of the best ginger pickles I ever tasted was the simplest. It consisted of thinly sliced fresh ginger marinated in cider vinegar in a glass bottle in the sun for ten days. A few slices will add some fireworks to any bland meal.

A more traditional Indian ginger chutney is prepared with the following ingredients:

    400 g fresh ginger
    300 g peeled garlic cloves
    2 tablespoons mustard seeds
    2 teaspoons chilli powder
    2 teaspoons salt
    200 g brown sugar
    250 g vinegar
    1 teaspoonful cumin seeds

Pound the ginger and garlic. Lightly fry the mustard seeds in a tablespoon or two of mustard oil or sesame oil. Mix everything and cook gently until it is all soft, and bottle when cool.

Anyone who has been to South India will have fallen in love with the fresh coconut chutneys. One simple recipe calls for grated coconut and chopped ginger in a ratio of about 4:1. To this is added chopped coriander leaves, green chillies and a little salt. The whole is wetted with lemon or lime juice, or with yoghurt, and mixed to a paste before chilling and serving.

A fresh tomato chutney requires:

    500 g tomatoes
    Grated rind from a lemon or a lime
    1 teaspoon coarsely ground black pepper
    5 cm piece of fresh ginger, chopped and crushed

113

¼ teaspoon chopped basil leaves
¼ teaspoon each paprika and turmeric

Boil or grill the tomatoes, and then pound together with all the other ingredients.

A carrot pickle is cheap and easy and will also need its ginger:

1 Kg carrots
6 minced garlic cloves
2 tablespoons ground mustard seed
2 teaspoons cumin seed
2 teaspoons powdered ginger
1 tablespoon coarsely ground peppercorns
250 g chopped green or red sweet peppers
Vinegar

Partly boil and chop the carrots, and sprinkle with salt. Leave for a day, then add all the other ingredients and cover with vinegar. It will be ready after a few days, when the carrots will have softened and taken up the spicy taste.

We shall leave the cooking at this point, happy to know that this chapter may have whetted some appetites. The process of cooking is an alchemy, just like the preparation of medicines. It blends qualities and elements from nature to achieve a satisfying effect on us, in this case on our stomachs. One way or another it is ginger's natural destination.

CHAPTER 10

Conclusion

Despite the last chapter's devotion to cakes and ale, the main purpose of this book is to teach us to take ginger more seriously. During this century ginger has been in a pickle in more ways than one. Relegated to the spice shelves, old and dried, ignored in household health care, without value, we have all but lost the knowledge of how to use it. Ginger has become something used in ginger ale and ginger biscuits, and it would seem incredible to many that lengthy and sophisticated treatises have been written in Chinese medicine and Indian traditional medicine about how best to use ginger to heal all kinds of conditions, some of them serious.

But now we can begin to see that we were ignorant. There is a seemingly endless knowledge of how to use ginger in health and disease, for a wide variety of ailments. It starts with straightforward information on the properties of the plant and its capability to treat specific health problems, with its constituents, with what other remedies it is classified from the therapeutic and chemical constituent points of view, and the connections between them. It continues with the more subtle art of knowing how best to use the plant for its energetic qualities—that is, its healing, cooling, energising, moving, stimulating and other effects, and how these work in the different organ systems of the body. There is the deep knowledge of using the herb differently with different kinds of people, who manifest health problems in different ways. Finally there is the ancient knowledge of how the herb combines in mixtures with other herbs, so that each complements the other, in special combinations designed for each health situation.

All this just about ginger. Then consider that there may be several thousand other herbal and mineral remedies to learn about. Readers of this book will no longer, I hope, be able to take the attitude that ginger and other spices are relatively irrelevant and uninteresting, and fit only to perk up the occasional curry.

So the potential knowledge is immense. No wonder a Chinese herbalist had to study for fifty years before he was recognised as a true master of his trade. This may sound rather daunting or discouraging. Who can grasp all this information? Does everyone have to study for fifty years before treating a cold?

Today there are few indeed who are fully masters in that sense. Instead, aspects of this information are being avidly collected by more modern-minded herbalists and researchers. In addition, there is a groundswell of interest among the general population who want to learn simple, useful measures, which will enable them to have and use a well stocked herbal first aid kit. In other words, all of us are somewhere in between the master herbalist and the innocent questioner who is amazed that one can write, or read, a whole book on ginger. Having a good store of information on ginger, perhaps more than one can directly use, increases the general network of such herbal lore within our culture, a kind of invisible archive of health care practices which can be drawn on more and more.

Taking it Home

Having read a whole book on ginger, it is possible to ignore it all as another fashionable health curiosity. Or to see ginger as useful only to those strange folk who have the time to mess around with things like ginger compresses. Or to decide to take ginger now and then for the occasional tummy upset or winter chill; or go the whole hog and treat is as a new discovery that opens up other dimensions of self-care and holistic living.

If this seems a bit far-fetched, then let us look again at the main uses for ginger that we have discussed. It is the best-known remedy for nausea, vomiting and stomach upsets, something that we all experience at times. It has an important use in a variety of other digestive disturbances, from indigestion to constipation. It stimulates the circulation, bringing warmth and life back into cold and congested body systems. It stimulates the heart and thins the blood. It helps to treat chronic low-grade infections and fevers. It is helpful in warming the lungs and chest and getting rid of colds, catarrh and bronchial problems. It reduces toxicity, burns up poisons in the body, and can aid rheumatic and menstrual disturbances. In addition it will help with the absorption of foods and other medicines.

The power of ginger continues with its culinary use. Besides bringing an aromatic vitality to a multitude of foods and drinks, it helps the digestion and absorption of foods which it accompanies, it is an anti-oxidant, it purifies the body of any toxins which might have crept in with the food, it reduces the amount of cholesterol being absorbed, and it protects the stomach.

All this is quite remarkable from a single medicinal food. Then consider that it is only one of a number of medicinal foods that you will find in the average kitchen, each of which may have a similar range of potential uses. Garlic, onion, turmeric, cayenne pepper, mint and fenugreek are typical examples. These are all windows of opportunities—'kitchen windows'—into a whole world of considerable interest and vitality.

The more we use them and know about them, the farther we go into a fascinating world where we relate much more fully to the things we consume. We learn how to gain better health and well-being. We can become busy in all kinds of internal experiments, rather like the ancient alchemists, trying out exactly when and how these herbs and medicinal foods help us. And a kaléidoscope of tastes and aromas opens in our cooking and handling of foods, plants and herbs. Above all, we gain extra control over our lives; we can design and use our own flavours and medicines, which can be a source of great joy and security.

This last statement needs some explanation. When you go to the doctor, say with chronic bronchitis or with angina pectoris or high blood pressure, you put yourself in the hands of a professional. He will use a language and techniques which are nothing to do with you, for example drugs whose names you can't even pronounce. You become a patient, and begin to feel like one. In a subtle way you lose control over the most important thing in your life, namely your health and feeling of well-being. On the other hand, if you get busy working on yourself, using some of the natural aids that are all around, you are out of that dependent category. The same goes for cooking. What you consume has a powerful long-term effect on your health. Yet most people resign this control to food manufacturers and food processors who cannot be said to have your personal well-being at the forefront of their minds. The result is not only dead and artificial foods that create a vast amount of disease, from allergies to cancer: more than that, a whole vital area of activity is lost from your control, and life becomes poorer thereby. The few extra minutes it takes to grate the ginger, and cook real, wholesome food, will return you to yourself and be richly rewarded.

So get busy with ginger. Add some fresh ginger to your vegetable rack. Put some in your medicine cabinet. Explore some of its uses, enjoy its possibilities, and then move on to the next herb and the next spice, and the next.

FURTHER READING

Herbal Guides

Tierra, M. *Planetary Herbology*. Lotus Press, Santa Fe, New Mexico (1988).

Holmes, P. *The Energetics of Western Herbs*. Artemis Press, POB 4295, Boulder, Colorado (1989).

Fawley, D. *Ayurvedic Healing*. Lotus Press, Santa Fe, New Mexico (1989).

Lal, V. *Ayurveda, The Science of Self-Healing*. Lotus Press, Santa Fe, New Mexico (1984).

Griggs, B. *Green Pharmacy, A History of Herbal Medicine*. Jill Norman & Hobhouse, London. Viking Press, New York (1982).

Grieve, M. *A Modern Herbal*. Penguin Books, London (1976).

Weiss, R. F. *Herbal Medicine*. Beaconsfield Publishers, Beaconsfield, Buckinghamshire (1988).

Mills, S. *Dictionary of Modern Herbalism*. Thorsons HarperCollins, London (1988).

Mills, S. *Out of the Earth: The Essential Book of Herbal Medicine*. Viking, London (1992).

Hsu, H-Y. and Peacher, W. G. *Chinese Herb Medicine and Therapy*. Oriental Healing Arts Institute, Los Angeles (1982).

Ginger Cooking

Seely, C. *Ginger Up Your Cookery*, Hutchinson Benham, London (1982).

Santa Maria, J. *Indian Vegetarian Cookery*. Rider, Century Hutchinson, London (1977).

Ginger, General, Agriculture, History, Chemistry

Govindarajan, V. S. 'Ginger—Chemistry, Technology and Quality Evaluation', CRC *Critical Reviews of Food Sciences and Nutrition*, **17**, 1–258 (1982).

Ilyas, M. 'The Spices of India', *Economic Botany*, **32**, 238–263 (1978).

Connell, D. W. 'The Chemistry of the Essential Oil and Oleoresin of Ginger (*Zingiber officinale* Roscoe)', *Flavour Industry*, **1**, 677–693 (1970).

Sakamura, F. 'Changes in Volatile Constituents of *Zingiber officinale* During Storage', *Phytochemistry*, **26**, 2207–2212 (1987).

Ginger, Pharmacology and Clinical Studies

Mowrey, D. B. and Claysion, D. E. 'Motion Sickness, Ginger and Psychophysics', *Lancet*, **1**, 655–657 (1982).

Grøntved, A. and Hentzer, E. 'Vertigo-Reducing Effects of Ginger Root', *ORL*, **48** 282–286 (1986).

Fischer-Rasmussen, W. *et al.* 'Ginger Treatment of Hyperemesis Gravidarum', *European J. Obstet. Gynaecol Reprod. Biol.*, **38**, 19–24 (1991).

Suekawa, M. *et al.* 'Pharmacological Studies in Ginger 1. Pharmacological Actions of Pungent Constituents (6)-gingerol and (6)-shogaol', *J. Pharm. Dyn.* **7**, 836–848 (1984).

Shoji, N. *et. al.*, 'Cardiotonic Principles of Ginger (*Zingiber officinale* Roscoe)', *J. Pharmaceutical Sciences*, **71**, 1174–5 (1982).

Mascob, N. *et. al.*, 'Ethnopharmacological Investigations on Ginger (*Zingiber officinale*)', *J. Ethnopharmacology*, **27**, 129–140 (1989).

Bone, M. E. *et. al.* 'Ginger in Postoperative Nausea and Vomiting', *Anaesthesia*, **45**, 669–671 (1990).

Atal, C. K. *et. al.* 'Scientific Evidence on the Role of Ayurvedic

Herbals on the Bioavailability of Drugs', *J. Ethnopharmacology*, **4**, 229–232 (1981).

Al-Yahya, M. A. *et. al.* 'Gastroprotective Activity of Ginger *Zingiber officinale* Rosc., in Rats', *Am. J. Chinese Medicine*, **17**, 51–56 (1989).

Gujral, S. *et. al.* 'Effect of Ginger (*Zingiber officinale* Roscoe) Oleoresin on Serum Cholesterol Levels in Cholesterol Fed Rats', *Nutrition Reports International*, **17**, 183–189 (1978).

Rattan, S. I. 'Science Behind the Spices: Inhibition of Platelet Aggregation and Prostaglandin Synthesis', *Bioessays*, **8**, 161–162 (1988).

Mustafa, T. and Srivastava, K. C. 'Ginger (*Zingiber officinale*) in Migraine Headache', *J. Ethnopharmacology*, **29**, 267–273 (1990).

Srivastava, K. *et. al.* 'Ginger and Rheumatic Disorders', *Medical Hypotheses*, **29**, 25–28 (1989).

General Self-Care

Fulder, S. *How to be a Healthy Patient*, Headway (Hodder & Stoughton), London (1991).

Mills, S. (Ed.) *Your Health, Your Choice*, Macmillan, London (1989).

Nightingale, M. *Holistic First Aid*, Optima, London (1988).

Dickenson, D. *How to Fortify Your Immune System*. Arlington, London (1982).

Bingham, S. *The Everyman Guide to Food and Nutrition*. Dent, London (1987).

Holford, P. *The Whole Health Manual*. Thorsons HarperCollins, London (1988).

Werbach, M. R. *Nutritional Influences on Illness*. Thorsons Harper-Collins, London (1989).

Collins, J. *Life Forces*. New English Library, London (1992).

NOTES

122

NOTES

NOTES

NOTES

NOTES

NOTES

NOTES